Imagining the Future of Undergraduate STEM Education

PROCEEDINGS OF A VIRTUAL SYMPOSIUM

Kerry Brenner, Alexandra Beatty, and Joe Alper, *Rapporteurs*

Board on Science Education

Board on Higher Education and Workforce

National Academy of Engineering

The National Academies of
SCIENCES · ENGINEERING · MEDICINE

THE NATIONAL ACADEMIES PRESS
Washington, DC
www.nap.edu

THE NATIONAL ACADEMIES PRESS 500 Fifth Street, NW Washington, DC 20001

This activity was supported by a contract between the National Academy of Sciences and the National Science Foundation (1935569). Any opinions, findings, conclusions, or recommendations expressed in this publication do not necessarily reflect the views of any organization or agency that provided support for the project.

International Standard Book Number–13: 978-0-309-09376-7
International Standard Book Number–10: 0-309-09376-7
Digital Object Identifier: https://doi.org/10.17226/26314

Additional copies of this publication are available from the National Academies Press, 500 Fifth Street, NW, Keck 360, Washington, DC 20001; (800) 624-6242 or (202) 334-3313; http://www.nap.edu.

Printed in the United States of America

Suggested citation: National Academies of Sciences, Engineering, and Medicine. 2022. *Imagining the Future of Undergraduate STEM Education: Proceedings of a Virtual Symposium.* Washington, DC: The National Academies Press. https://doi.org/10.17226/26314.

The National Academies of

SCIENCES • ENGINEERING • MEDICINE

The **National Academy of Sciences** was established in 1863 by an Act of Congress, signed by President Lincoln, as a private, nongovernmental institution to advise the nation on issues related to science and technology. Members are elected by their peers for outstanding contributions to research. Dr. Marcia McNutt is president.

The **National Academy of Engineering** was established in 1964 under the charter of the National Academy of Sciences to bring the practices of engineering to advising the nation. Members are elected by their peers for extraordinary contributions to engineering. Dr. John L. Anderson is president.

The **National Academy of Medicine** (formerly the Institute of Medicine) was established in 1970 under the charter of the National Academy of Sciences to advise the nation on medical and health issues. Members are elected by their peers for distinguished contributions to medicine and health. Dr. Victor J. Dzau is president.

The three Academies work together as the **National Academies of Sciences, Engineering, and Medicine** to provide independent, objective analysis and advice to the nation and conduct other activities to solve complex problems and inform public policy decisions. The National Academies also encourage education and research, recognize outstanding contributions to knowledge, and increase public understanding in matters of science, engineering, and medicine.

Learn more about the National Academies of Sciences, Engineering, and Medicine at **www.nationalacademies.org**.

The National Academies of

SCIENCES • ENGINEERING • MEDICINE

Consensus Study Reports published by the National Academies of Sciences, Engineering, and Medicine document the evidence-based consensus on the study's statement of task by an authoring committee of experts. Reports typically include findings, conclusions, and recommendations based on information gathered by the committee and the committee's deliberations. Each report has been subjected to a rigorous and independent peer-review process and it represents the position of the National Academies on the statement of task.

Proceedings published by the National Academies of Sciences, Engineering, and Medicine chronicle the presentations and discussions at a workshop, symposium, or other event convened by the National Academies. The statements and opinions contained in proceedings are those of the participants and are not endorsed by other participants, the planning committee, or the National Academies.

For information about other products and activities of the National Academies, please visit www.nationalacademies.org/about/whatwedo.

PLANNING COMMITTEE FOR A SYMPOSIUM ON IMAGINING THE FUTURE OF UNDERGRADUATE EDUCATION[1]

ANNETTE PARKER (*Co-chair*), South Central College
BARBARA SCHAAL (*Co-chair*), Washington University in St. Louis
LEANNE CHUKOSKIE, Qualcomm Institute, University of California, San Diego
KINNIS GOSHA, Morehouse College
NICHOLAS HORTON, Amherst College
RYAN KELSEY, Markle Foundation
KIRK KOLENBRANDER, Southern New Hampshire University
ARTHUR LEE, Chevron Services Company
CATHRYN MANDUCA, Carleton College
CHRISTINE ORTIZ, MIT, Station1
JOSIPA ROKSA, University of Virginia
LYNN A. STEIN, Olin College
MONIQUE UMPHREY, Houston Community College, Northeast

Project Staff

KERRY BRENNER, *Senior Program Officer*
ELIZABETH T. CADY, *Senior Program Officer*
TIFFANY E. TAYLOR, *Program Officer*
LETICIA GARCILAZO GREEN, *Research Associate*
LAYNE SCHERER, *Senior Program Officer*
ELIZABETH SUMERLIN, *Senior Program Assistant*
IVORY DEAN, *Program Officer*
ALEXANDRA BEATTY, *Senior Program Officer*
HEIDI SCHWEINGRUBER, *Senior Board Director*

JOE ALPER, *Consulting Writer*

[1]The National Academies of Sciences, Engineering, and Medicine's planning committees are solely responsible for organizing the workshop, identifying topics, and choosing speakers. The responsibility for the published Proceedings of a Workshop rests with the workshop rapporteurs and the institution.

BOARD ON HIGHER EDUCATION AND WORKFORCE

Acknowledgments

The National Academies of Sciences, Engineering, and Medicine's Board on Science Education and Board on Higher Education and Workforce thank the National Science Foundation for its support of this symposium and wish to express their sincere gratitude to the planning committee co-chairs Annette Parker and Barbara Schaal for their valuable contributions to the development and orchestration of this virtual symposium. We also wish to thank all the members of the planning committee, who collaborated to ensure a symposium complete with informative presentations and rich discussions. Finally, we want to thank the speakers and moderators, who generously shared their expertise and their time with symposium participants.

This Proceedings of a Symposium was reviewed in draft form by individuals chosen for their diverse perspectives and technical expertise. The purpose of this independent review is to provide candid and critical comments that will assist the National Academies of Sciences, Engineering, and Medicine in making each published proceedings as sound as possible and to ensure that it meets the institutional standards for quality, objectivity, evidence, and responsiveness to the charge. The review comments and draft manuscript remain confidential to protect the integrity of the process.

We thank the following individuals for their review of this proceedings: Margaret E. Beier, Department of Psychological Sciences, Rice University, and James E. Swartz, Center for Science and the Liberal Arts, Grinnell College.

Although the reviewers listed above provided many constructive comments and suggestions, they were not asked to endorse the content of the proceedings nor did they see the final draft before its release. The review of this proceedings was overseen by Emily Miller. She was responsible for making certain that an independent examination of this proceedings was carried out in accordance with standards of the National Academies and that all review comments were carefully considered. Responsibility for the final content rests entirely with the rapporteurs and the National Academies.

Contents

Boxes, Figures, and Table

BOXES

FIGURES

TABLE

Acronyms and Abbreviations

ADL	U.S. Government's Advanced Distributed Learning Program
ANAPISI	Asian American, Native American, and Pacific Islander-Serving Institution
HBCU	Historically Black College and University
HSI	Hispanic-Serving Institution
MSI	Minority-Serving Institution
NSF	National Science Foundation
SACNAS	Society for Advancement of Chicanos/Hispanics and Native Americans in Science
STEM	Science, Technology, Engineering, and Mathematics

1

Introduction

What do you imagine the world will be like in 2040? What technology will we have come to take for granted? What will be the most pressing threats to the health of Earth and the health of humanity? What kinds of things will scientists be researching? And what tools will they be using in their research? What will the scientists and engineers of the future look like? How will they learn the skills, practices, and concepts they need to contribute to innovation? Will undergraduate education have changed to better prepare students for their lives and careers? Will students of all races, ethnicities, cultures, perspectives, and backgrounds feel welcome in the classrooms and other learning environments of 2040? Will undergraduate education prepare all students to use scientific thinking and science, technology, engineering, and mathematics (STEM) skills in their lives and careers, regardless of whether they become STEM professionals?

In November 2020, the National Academies of Sciences, Engineering, and Medicine convened a multiday virtual symposium on imaging the future of undergraduate STEM education. Speakers and participants grappled with the issues underlying the questions above. They pondered the future and the past, they shared their goals, priorities, and dreams for improving undergraduate STEM education, and they were encouraged to think outside the box and offer opinions based on their own experiences with higher education. Expert speakers presented information about today's students and approaches to undergraduate STEM education, as well as the history of transformation in higher education. Thoughtful discussions explored ideas for the future, how student-centered learning experiences could be created, and what issues to consider to facilitate a successful transformation.

Institutions are under pressure because of resource constraints, new demands for accountability, and the need to adapt to new research on learning and instruction. STEM fields themselves are developing at a rapid pace, boosted by technological advances such as "big data" and the new possibilities for automation. Institutions are also increasingly focused on the importance of equity and inclusion and the different ways of serving undergraduate learners who are more diverse than ever in regard to their personal characteristics, background, preparation, interests, and goals. Nationwide, not all segments of the U.S. population—women, people of color, people of low socioeconomic status, people with disabilities, LGBTQ+ individuals, and others—are reaping the benefits of high-quality STEM education, and they remain underrepresented among those students completing undergraduate STEM baccalaureate programs. Students from those groups disproportionately either switch to non-STEM majors during their education or drop out of college, and they are thus even less well represented in STEM jobs and graduate-level STEM programs. Over the next several decades, though, job openings requiring STEM skills are expected to grow more than twice as fast as non-STEM occupations and to pay better than non-STEM jobs (Bureau of Labor Statistics, 2020; Smithsonian Institution, 2021). Employers seek graduates with transferable skills, such as creativity and adaptability, as well as skills in teamwork, communication, conflict resolution, and problem solving. To thrive in the coming decades, workers will need to be prepared to adapt and switch gears. People in jobs not traditionally thought of as STEM jobs will increasingly need STEM skills to be effective. STEM skills will be required to navigate not only the expected wider array of jobs and careers in the working world, but also to enable wider participation in democracy, and as people make decisions in their daily lives.

The COVID-19 pandemic forced U.S. colleges and universities to dramatically alter the way they educated the nation's undergraduates and highlighted many underlying issues of undergraduate education that had already been simmering. It required the rethinking of approaches to undergraduate learning and prompted some to question their own assumptions. It spurred others to focus more deeply on new approaches to undergraduate STEM education. In this context, the National Academies of Sciences, Engineering, and Medicine, with support from the National Science Foundation (NSF), held a public symposium on the future of undergraduate STEM education. The symposium was designed to visualize a post-pandemic world and explore possibilities for undergraduate STEM education in 2040 and beyond in the context of the convergence of STEM disciplines and the changes in the demographic makeup, goals, and educational pathways of undergraduate STEM students. The charge to the committee was to organize an event that addressed the following questions:

- How can undergraduate STEM education respond to the rapidly changing context for higher education—calls for convergence, demographic and societal changes, changes in workforce demands, and advances in technology—in ways that anticipate future demands and provide quality education for all students?
- What changes are needed to undergraduate STEM education in light of the increasing convergence across STEM disciplines? What are critical convergent topics and approaches that we urgently need to incorporate into undergraduate STEM education?
- What are the models, both administrative and financial, that support a convergent learning experience that engages multiple disciplines and overarching concerns such as privacy, security, and the ethical behavior of people and systems?
- Is there a relationship between the content, delivery mechanism, and use of technology in the classroom/learning environment and the success of first-generation and low-income STEM students of all backgrounds? Is the relationship different for different groups? What would it mean to design changes based on an equity and social justice mindset from the start?
- How should the STEM education system respond to the changes taking place in the learning pathways of individuals at different points of their lives, including enrolling at different physical and online institutions, and/or stacking credentials and experiences from multiple sources? How can we consider learning in contexts other than formal settings for different cultures, ages, or levels of instruction?

STRUCTURE OF THE SYMPOSIUM AND THE PROCEEDINGS

The symposium planning committee, whose role was confined to planning and organizing the agenda and event, included educators and administrators from a range of disciplines and types of institutions who had demonstrated innovative approaches to thinking about undergraduate STEM education. They convened multiple times to grapple with the questions in their charge and plan an event that would stimulate participants to imagine undergraduate STEM education in 2040. As they worked to identify, invite, and provide guidance to the speakers, the committee had to make multiple decisions about how to interpret their charge. It was not feasible to answer some of the thought-provoking questions posed to them at this time, so the committee organized an array of activities to engage experts and stakeholders with diverse perspectives in discussing the underlying issues and related ideas. The committee chose to define convergence inclusively and to consider interdisciplinary, multidisciplinary, and other approaches to integrating real-world challenges and issues into student learning experiences. They provided multiple opportunities for participants to engage in the symposium topics before and during the live, webcast symposium.

Before the symposium, a wide-ranging call went out to educators to participate in an idea competition by submitting a statement or video addressing some aspect of the symposium's focus on what undergraduate STEM education should look like in 2040 and beyond to meet the needs of students, science, and society and what we should do now to prepare. Winning submissions were on the National Academies website, and many were discussed at the symposium.[1] In addition, the committee commissioned two papers to be presented at the symposium that were posted on the project website in advance. Moderated discussion boards allowed participants to discuss themes emerging from the idea competition and the papers in preparation for the symposium and continue to discuss topics arising during the symposium itself. The 3-day symposium included presentations and discussion of the two papers, panel discussions, and break-out sessions to generate ideas and develop individual stories to represent visions for the future (the agenda appears in Appendix B).

This proceedings, which was prepared by the workshop rapporteurs, summarizes the presentations and ideas that were articulated during the symposium. A key purpose of the symposium was to provide participants with multiple opportunities to explore and share ideas from varied perspectives. To make it easier for the reader to follow the discussion threads, this report clusters the account of the proceedings into categories corresponding to themes that predominated throughout the symposium. Chapter 2 discusses the purposes of STEM education and goals for the future. Chapter 3 presents the commissioned paper on "Transformation in the U.S. Higher Education System: Implications for Racial Equity" by Lindsey Malcom-Piqueux. Chapter 4 presents research on today's diverse undergraduate students, while Chapter 5 discusses ways to create equitable opportunities for future undergraduate students. Chapter 6 discusses changes in technology, Chapter 7 presents the commissioned paper "Current Innovations in STEM Education and Equity Needs for the Future" by Katerina Bagiati and Sanjay Sarma, as well as other innovative strategies and approaches for improving undergraduate STEM education. Lastly, Chapter 8 summarizes the broad reflections and final thoughts that were put forward at the symposium.

[1] See https://www.nationalacademies.org/our-work/idea-competition-for-Symposium-on-imagining-the-future-of-undergraduate-stem-education.

OBJECTIVES FOR THE SYMPOSIUM

Symposium participants were asked to visualize what society and science will look like in 2040, the future date at which many babies born during the pandemic will be engaged in undergraduate education, noted National Academy of Sciences' President Marcia McNutt in her welcoming remarks. She suggested that remarkable shifts in the delivery of undergraduate pedagogy can be expected in the next 20 years and asked participants to consider what changes could create a more inclusive environment in which women, people of color, and people from groups that are currently underrepresented in the STEM disciplines will have full access to the opportunities a STEM degree creates. McNutt also pointed to the consequences of failing to adapt, noting that "we need STEM education to be available everywhere and available to everyone. We must rethink many of our traditional approaches." She noted that STEM education has evolved to include more inquiry-based learning that emphasizes fewer lectures and more hands-on time in the classroom, and that these types of learning experiences need to become accessible to a wider variety of students. Engaging students in making sense of the world around them by asking questions, gathering data, analyzing evidence, and learning to communicate their ideas, results, and conclusions teaches them both about STEM and how STEM works, she emphasized. She concluded, "I do not know a single kid who is not curious, and yet, so many of our STEM classes almost beat the curiosity out of them."

Others also offered thoughts about the goals for the symposium and the importance of STEM and STEM education: Sethuraman Panchanathan, director of NSF; F. Fleming Crim, chief operating officer for NSF; Karen Marrongelle, head of NSF's Directorate for Education and Human Resources; and planning committee co-chairs Annette Parker, president of South Central College, and Barbara Schaal, the Mary Dell Chilton distinguished professor at Washington University in St. Louis.

NSF sees undergraduate STEM education as key to its vision: advancing the frontiers of research, ensuring accessibility and inclusivity, and securing global leadership in STEM, Crim explained. "Ensuring accessibility and inclusivity is the base on which the other two pillars rest," he added. Marrongelle commented on the unprecedented speed with which changes to the STEM research and education landscape are occurring. She noted that these changes are enabled by advances in computer and engineering technologies such as artificial intelligence and robotics and that they are also enabled by a deeper understanding of societal and environmental change, along with very important advances in the learning sciences. She also pointed out the changing conceptions of both work and the workplace enabled by intelligent and autonomous systems. She described a vision for the future that is "powered by evidence-based instruction and technology to maximize STEM learning and mitigate barriers, including cost, distance, opportunity, socioeconomic background, and prior STEM preparation." She also explained how this vision must be aligned with the ways students learn across different contexts and life stages and how it needs to be personalized, project-based, and learner-centered to aid students in tackling real-life STEM problems, including those in their communities. She argued that building this vision for the future means that we need to systemically implement curricular innovations and effective practices in STEM education. She further commented that "at the core of our thinking, we must figure out how to move into a future STEM that is more equitable, diverse, and inclusive."

Schaal observed that a strong STEM education could help citizens navigate through the cacophony of voices in the public sphere and develop informed opinions about issues such as the relative wisdom of eating or avoiding genetically modified foods, vaccinating children (or not), and the reality (or unreality) of climate change. STEM should be part of a general education, she commented, for "the vast diversity of our citizens, not just one component of our citizenry." Parker asked the symposium participants to imagine a future where undergraduate STEM education serves students well, saying, "We want you to explore strategies for imagining new approaches, including restructuring curriculum, majors, departments, credentials, and institutions, and we want you to think about all the potential scientists who have been excluded from STEM."

2

Goals for the Future: Changing Purposes of Undergraduate STEM Education

What purposes does undergraduate science, technology, engineering, and mathematics (STEM) education currently serve? How is it likely to change, and how should it change? Four panelists were asked to consider the role of STEM education in helping students to become effective citizens of a democracy and prepared to contribute to the workforce (see Box 2-1). Panelists were chosen to provide perspectives on the purpose of undergraduate STEM education from their view points in industry, and at a Community College, a liberal arts college, and a research university. They were asked to consider the diverse contributions that STEM fields make to society and how those contributions might shape priorities for STEM education.

GOALS OF UNDERGRADUATE STEM EDUCATION

University of South Carolina provost William Tate opened the panel by calling on higher education to democratize access to information and knowledge, including increasing opportunities for access to the best teachers and to evidence-based learning experiences. He particularly pointed out the need to pay attention to the realm of "computational tools and artificial intelligence as it relates to the very fabric of our society." He observed that these tools affect both legal, health, and medicine systems, and that a key function of STEM education is to provide all students the opportunity to understand these tools and their role in a democracy. All students need access to the very best programming and teachers, accessed using whatever platform works best.

BOX 2-1
Goals for the Future

What purposes does undergraduate STEM education serve now and how should that change in the future?

Panelists:
Eloy Oakley, Chancellor, California Community College System
Wanda Sigur, Former Vice President and Deputy General Manager, Lockheed Martin Space Systems' Civil Space business (retired)
Francis Su, Benediktsson-Karwa Professor of Mathematics, Harvey Mudd College
William F. Tate IV, Provost, University of South Carolina

Moderators:
Arthur Lee, Fellow and Principal Advisor, Chevron Services Company, committee member
Cathy Manduca, Director, Science Education Resource Center, Carleton College, committee member

Oakley drew on his experience as chancellor of the California Community College system, which, he noted, educates one of every four Community College students in the nation. The system provides training and education for a substantial fraction of the nation's nurses and other allied health professionals. Community Colleges, in his view, are critical to democratizing access to STEM fields because they place a strong emphasis on access and inclusion. "This is the place where so many students of all backgrounds can come to pursue careers in STEM fields," he noted. These institutions also have the opportunity to form partnerships with 4-year institutions and employers that are important means of diversifying the STEM workforce. The challenge, in his view, is for Community Colleges to do a better job of making students aware of the pathways into STEM fields and to do so with urgency in this "moment of racial reckoning." He added, "It is not just critical for the students that want to pursue these pathways, it is critical for us as a nation to begin to diversify these fields and to really show students that they can see themselves as doctors, as nurses, as biotech professionals, as computer engineers."

From Sigur's perspective in industry, the primary purpose of undergraduate STEM education is to act as a bridge for K–12 students to further STEM education and careers. Perhaps the most important goal of undergraduate STEM education in her view is that students gain critical thinking skills, which can often happen through experiential learning. She agreed with Tate that understanding computer science and technology is both key and becoming increasingly accessible, and consequently, undergraduate STEM education needs to keep preparing students adequately. "Changes . . . in health care, robotics, and artificial intelligence are going to change the world," she noted, and this will influence expectations for STEM careers.

Sigur also emphasized that innovation requires a diversity of thought. Increasingly, she suggested, industries that rely on STEM professionals will look to race-conscious, inclusive institutions as places that generate diverse ideas. The demand for innovation will work to the benefit of universities that take advantage of virtual learning to pursue such goals as introducing students to international collaborations, in her view. Expanded partnerships with industry can provide students with valuable opportunities for experiential learning, she noted. Postsecondary institutions that embrace the connections between STEM fields and the arts and humanities, she added, will also contribute to enhancing student capacities for innovative thinking.

Su, a mathematics professor at Harvey Mudd College, began by explaining the difference between skills, which are things for students to learn, and virtues and character traits built by education. Virtues include "persistence, curiosity, creativity, intellectual humility" and the confidence to tackle new problems. Higher education focuses on skills because they are easier to assess than virtues, but skills can be replaced by computers or artificial intelligence. Virtues, however, will always be in demand, and a broader focus on virtues will make equity easier to achieve. "These virtues will serve you well no matter what profession you go into, no matter where your life takes you, and make your life richer," Su said, adding that while necessary skills change often, virtues drive innovation. Consequently, he believes that "the most important goal of a STEM education in 2040 is the same as it is today: the development of virtue and also broadening how we think about education to address it."

GOALS FOR UNDERGRADUATE STEM LEARNING

Planning committee member Cathy Manduca noted that she heard three "big classes of goals in the opening statements" made by the panelists. She summarized Tate's comments about the importance of preparing students to be democratic citizens, ensuring that all students understand the role of technology and STEM in our society, ensuring that they understand how it impacts our lives as citizens. She reiterated Sigur's and Oakley's observations about the preparation of the workforce, and then finally, Su's comments about the importance of higher education in creating individuals who flourish as human beings. Stating that she believes that these are broad and rich goals for higher education, she asked the panelists to talk about the "relationships between these goals and how prioritizing one or another might suggest a different future for undergraduate STEM learning or how they can be brought together in ways that allow all these goals to flourish."

Tate views the goals articulated by Manduca as interdependent and not mutually exclusive. In his view, access that begins in the K–12 environment and at Community Colleges is the foundation for both creating a STEM-literate citizenry and democratizing the ways in which STEM plays out in U.S. society. Tate added that those who will be designing new technologies and Artificial Intelligence (AI) tools should learn virtues in their education that could address potential "disparities [that] might unfold in the technology we use." Sigur agreed that these three goals are interdependent, and that developing virtues is part of "shaping a mind, establishing expectations, and enabling a STEM worker to be agile and able to handle" all the new ideas and concepts that will crop up in 2040 and beyond.

Oakley also agreed with the importance of developing virtues, but he highlighted the challenge of addressing the systemic issues of discrimination and racism embedded in the educational system that prevent communities of color and low-income communities from accessing STEM jobs. "Hiring processes that exist," said Oakley, "do not hire on the basis of virtue. They hire on the basis of where you went to school for the top engineering jobs in the country, or if you want to become a doctor or if you want to get a fellowship. So we need to think about how we set up a system that values the kinds of virtues that we're talking about and does not continue to value the kinds of barriers that we put up as a system of higher education," including the barriers that exist because of the current math curriculum." In Oakley's experience, students from low-income or difficult backgrounds are highly creative and resilient problem-solvers, and they need the opportunity to demonstrate those virtues in the STEM fields.

Su said that he avoids talking about education as a means to get a job and instead focuses on developing the whole person in terms of character, compassion, and community-centered learning. Experiential learning is a critical piece of education, and Su explained that educators need to teach students how to interact with people from completely different backgrounds and learn to appreciate their strengths, which traditional assessments often miss. "What I hope will happen by 2040 is that we could imagine an educational system where people actually think about issues of justice, think about issues that are affecting their particular communities," said Su. "We have to think about how to shape [learning] experiences so that students see themselves in those experiences and are able to fully participate in them."

The Role of Internships

From his perspective as a hiring manager, planning committee member Arthur Lee asked the panelists to comment on the value that employers can get from experiential learning and the role that internships and co-ops play in undergraduate STEM education. He also asked the panelists to address those aspects of STEM education that employers would most value today and in the future. Oakley remarked that there is a need to put less value on a degree and more on competency, experiences, and skills. The value we give to higher education should not be based on who attends selective universities; higher education should be valued for "creating the greatest opportunity for the largest amount of individuals, and then rethinking the way that we communicate those skills." Achieving that state will require building portfolios of student experiences and demonstrated skills and competencies rather than rewarding degrees from specific institutions.

Sigur noted that the aerospace industry does not consider a prospective employee's school as a primary criterion for hiring, but looks for people with experiences in applying learned information who can become specialists with on-the-job training. "Frankly," she said, "you get an opportunity to develop critical thinking only as you start to apply the things you have learned in school." She added that when she, a Black girl in New Orleans, decided she wanted to be an engineer, she had no idea what an engineering degree really involved nor a complete understanding of what working in the engineering field would entail. The co-op experience required her to use skills and approaches that she had learned in school to analyze data and resolve issues. It "forced me to understand the importance of critical thinking," she said, "and the dance between working and going back to school allowed me to pull for answers that I wouldn't have otherwise pulled for and frankly shaped my ability to be successful in the working world." Sigur added that although hiring managers in her industry consider an applicant's university degree and their course work, "it is even more important to see whether or not someone already has the ability to perform, because more than anything, you would like to have someone show up on day one and be able to execute."

Tate explained that programs that have democratized access provide students with the opportunity to experience research and enhance their research skills and also provide mentors and a comprehensive support system, and they enable access to both professional networks outside of the university ecosystem and socialization into their chosen STEM fields. "That screams co-op, an opportunity to work in industry, and undergraduate research," said Tate. "It screams that the link between undergraduate research and going out into the professional work world is extremely important." He added that the discussion should stop being about degrees and instead focus on programs—both in 2-year and 4-year institutions—and the question of whether a program of study includes the type of virtues that Su identified. "If we are doing that, we are going to have great students," said Tate.

Su agreed that experiential learning is "hugely important," regardless of whether it comes from being in the workforce, having an internship with a company, or working in an academic laboratory. In fact, he called for institutions of higher education to restructure their curricula to feature fewer lectures and more hands-on experiences. He noted that the COVID-19 pandemic, with its heavy reliance on online education, has cost students the opportunity to have these in-person, hands-on experiences that not only teach skills, but also allow them to see how people treat each other in academic and nonacademic settings.

TRANSFORMING STRUCTURES OF UNDERGRADUATE STEM EDUCATION

Setting the stage for upcoming symposium panels focused on the transformation of undergraduate education, Manduca then asked the panelists to speak about what the ideal future educational structures will look like. Su said he sees higher education taking advantage of online platforms to have courses taught by the best teachers, but also including in-person, experiential learning, possibly using flipped learning models. Oakley commented that it is difficult to imagine how any new structure for STEM education works without universal access to broadband internet, an element of infrastructure that is becoming an increasingly fundamental stepping stone toward achieving many of these aspirational goals. The other critical infrastructure piece needed is diversifying faculty and staff so that students can see themselves in their instructors and faculty can better understand the experiences of their students. STEM educators of color or those who come from low-income backgrounds can help build underlying education infrastructure, said Oakley.

Structures of higher education that currently act as barriers were also discussed by the panelists, one example being that math courses can act as gatekeepers and limit who can enroll in other STEM courses. Oakley mentioned how algebra is often taught as a bunch of rote things you have to memorize without context. He called on curriculum designers in the higher education environment to think about how to make these experiences more relevant to the lives of students and enable students to more fully participate. Sigur pointed out the need to be creative and support and encourage students from diverse backgrounds who may not come in with a strength in algebra. She explained the need for a more intense focus on experiential learning so that students leave higher education ready to produce and perform on day one of their employment. Oakley, with his perspective from Community Colleges, explained that many students from low-income communities, students who have come from very difficult backgrounds, are often the most creative: they are great problem-solvers and amazingly resilient, so we need to give them an opportunity to demonstrate those skills, to demonstrate those virtues in the kind of jobs that we are talking about. He said that "we as educators need to find a better way to measure the kinds of learning that we think we are going to need to support our students with as they get into the fields of the future." Su commented that he shies away from focusing on getting a job as the purpose of education because he does not want people to think about education as a competition. He encouraged a larger focus on developing the whole person in relation to compassion, character, and in all things, taking into account our fellow students, the people that we are learning with together in community. He pointed out that a focus on experiential learning has got to be a huge part of that.

Tate noted that at research universities like his every department has some faculty or staff who excel in the big class lecture format and others who are outstanding at teaching small classes and providing one-on-one instruction, yet academia has never organized instructional responsibilities in a way that builds on the assets and strengths of their individual faculty members. In his opinion, this type of organization could help increase persistence toward STEM degrees simply by reducing the chances that students will have one or two bad instructional experiences. Sigur added that, given the costs of higher education, "there will be a greater pull for schools getting better and being responsive as people consider that it's not just an investment of time anymore but of significant dollars." Finally, Su commented that he was hoping "that as we move forward, people will begin to see some of the most important things about college education aren't necessarily just the physical surroundings and the perks that you get. What's really essential, I think, is the community that you build and that you learn together now."

SUMMARY

To close the discussion period, Lee, speaking as a STEM businessperson, addressed the question as to why more employers do not offer internships by saying that there has to be a business case for investing in an internship program so the company can see a future benefit. Manduca began her summary of the discussion by stressing "these three goals of developing virtuous students able to have rich lives, of creating a citizenry that is prepared for our democracy and for living in it, and creating a workforce for tomorrow." Education works best when it serves all those goals together, she observed. She also highlighted the discussions of virtues within the workforce, valuing programs over degrees, and the community one builds in education. Finally, Manduca ended the session by reiterating Tate's remarks about the importance of a student's networks inside and outside of their education and the fact that community includes not only fellow students but also the faculty and the people a student engages with as they go into the world through experiential learning. "That is, I think, a really lovely vision," Manduca said, "and it really sets up this notion that in the future, we will have new roles and mixtures of ways of learning. I like the idea that the graduate students and the faculty all form a community of learning that maximizes both the learning for the students and the capabilities of the members of that community."

3

Transformation in the U.S. Higher Education System

In considering how to transform undergraduate STEM education for 2040, pausing to reflect on past efforts at transformation in higher education can be informative. What were the goals of previous efforts? What were the outcomes? What assumptions and expectations drove the thinking behind them? What assumptions and expectations influenced the resulting actions? What changed and what remained resistant to change?

Lindsey Malcom-Piqueux authored and presented a paper to symposium participants on "Transformation in the U.S. Higher Education System: Implications for Racial Equity," which examined key historical moments and provided a framework for using past experiences to structure positive change for the future.[1]

IMPLICATIONS FOR RACIAL EQUITY

Racial inequity is endemic to the U.S. higher education system, which is "not news to anyone who follows STEM education and employment," explained Malcom-Piqueux of Caltech. Students who are members of racially minoritized groups are more likely to attend college than in years past, but they still experience inequitable access to educational opportunity. She presented data showing that students of color are disproportionately attending Community Colleges and for-profit institutions rather than 4-year institutions (see Figure 3-1). As a result, students from

[1]A PDF of the paper is available at https://www.nationalacademies.org/event/10-21-2020/imagining-the-future-of-undergraduate-stem-education-symposium.

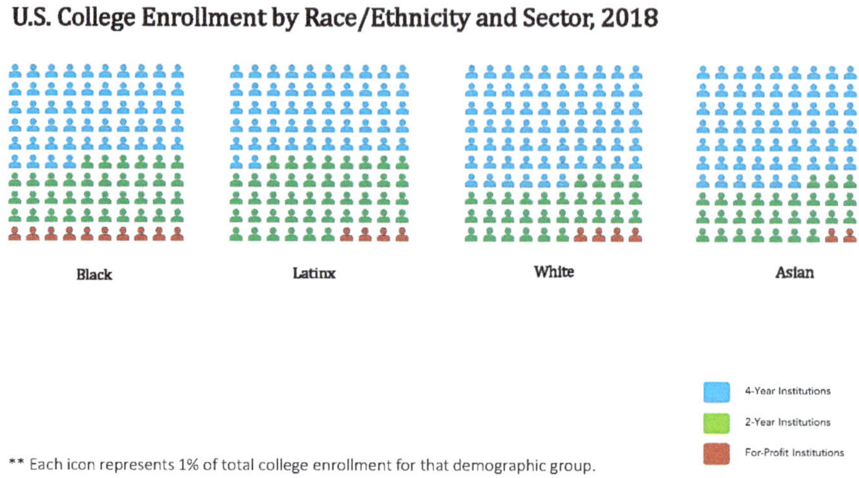

FIGURE 3-1 Racial stratification in higher education.
SOURCE: Malcom-Piqueux symposium slides.

these groups are concentrated in institutions that do not offer the same breadth of STEM curriculum and provide fewer opportunities to engage in authentic STEM learning.

The institutions in which students from racially minoritized groups are most likely to be enrolled do offer pathways to STEM careers, but the STEM students from these groups are more likely to switch out of STEM majors and take longer to complete bachelor's degrees. The effects of the challenges and constraints these students face are evident in the decreasing proportions of such students in master's and doctoral degree programs, Malcom-Piqueux noted.

Inequities in STEM education and higher education generally reflect the broader sociopolitical context in the United States, she explained. Racial discrimination that was codified into law to deny minorities economic and educational opportunities in decades past continues to affect the lives of those in marginalized groups. Although postsecondary enrollment has increased for these groups, highly stratified patterns of attendance are the continuing legacy of past discrimination and segregation. "It is the underlying intent and logic of those policies [that has] led to the conditions that we observe today," Malcom-Piqueux commented. She noted that researchers who have studied persistent underrepresentation point to the need to address the root causes of disparities in access and outcomes if STEM education is to be transformed.

THREE TRANSFORMATIONAL MOMENTS

Malcom-Piqueux analyzed three past efforts to expand access to higher education in the United States, which she called transformational moments, to gain insight into the complex motives for and effects of these efforts. Each in its own way, she explained, illustrates the lasting effects that policies, institutional actions, and beliefs about race in the United States have had on racial equity today.

The first of the three transformational developments was the passage of the Morrill Land Grant College Acts of 1862 and 1890, which created colleges that were to focus on military science, agriculture, and the mechanical arts (engineering). Through these acts, the federal government granted land, much of which belonged to dispossessed Native American tribes, to individual states, which could in turn sell the land in order to fund the establishment of the new colleges. Malcom-Piqueux pointed out that although the acts were explicitly intended to expand access to higher education, the new colleges admitted very few women, and African American students were permitted to attend only designated institutions (the original Historically Black Colleges and Universities, or HBCUs). Although the acts did provide new opportunities for African American students, the new institutions maintained racial segregation in practice, giving states ways to underfund those that served African American students even though the second of the two acts specifically required equitable distribution of funds.

A second U.S. effort to dramatically expand postsecondary access was the G.I. Bill (the Serviceman's Readjustment Act of 1944), which provided benefits, including tuition payments, to veterans of World War II. The G.I. Bill fueled a huge influx of enrollment in postsecondary institutions, including state colleges and universities, Community Colleges, and vocational schools, and for a minority of the returning veterans, elite institutions.

African-American G.I.s were eligible for these benefits, as Malcom-Piqueux explained, but the social context of the 1940s limited their access in practice. Many had attended racially segregated and under-resourced secondary schools and were not well prepared for college. They faced discriminatory admissions policies that restricted their access to many institutions, so Black G.I.s disproportionately enrolled in vocational programs or were not able to take advantage of the educational benefit at all. Even the chronically underfunded HBCUs turned away many G.I.s because they lacked sufficient resources to handle the influx. Additionally, many of those institutions lacked the accreditation necessary so that their graduates could be accepted at graduate and professional schools. Consequently, Malcom-Piqueux explained, the general widening of access accomplished by the G.I. Bill also had the effect of reinforcing racial stratification and inequality within higher education.

The third transformational event was the U.S. response to the launching of Sputnik I by the USSR in 1957. The U.S. government regarded this launch of the first human-made object into space as an indication of educational failure for the United States and immediately focused attention and funds on the goal of strengthening science research, public education, and workforce development. The National Defense Education Act (NDEA) of 1958 provided funds to the states to strengthen science education, a significant portion of which went to a small number of research universities to expand programs and facilities for research and development in science, engineering, and technology.

One goal of the NDEA was to foster equal access to high-quality science education, but as with the other two examples, Malcom-Piqueux explained, many people from racially minoritized populations were ultimately excluded from the benefits. The forms of aid available to students, the testing and guidance used to identify promising students for new programs, and continued support for segregated institutions, for example, all played a role in limiting the racial equity of the expanding education and research infrastructure.

THE EQUITY QUADRANT FRAMEWORK

Malcom-Piqueux presented the framework she used to analyze efforts such as the land grant acts, the G.I. Bill, and the NDEA in order to characterize their implications for racial equity in higher education, shown in Figure 3-2. The framework is modeled on a tool developed by the Center for Urban Education (CUE, 2020).

The quadrant uses two dimensions to assess policies that have effects on postsecondary opportunity for people from racially minoritized populations. The first dimension, policy intent, is a gauge of a policy's intended effect on equity, whether to promote inclusion or exclusion. The second, racial logic, is a gauge of how consciously the policy's designers tried to account for the effects of sociopolitical, historical, and cultural circumstances on the way the policies would operate in practice. Race-conscious policies, she explained, are those designed to reflect those realities, while race-neutral ones do not take into account racial attitudes. This second dimension, Malcom-Piqueux noted, could be either positive or negative, that is, it may identify the objective of fostering equity or of protecting racist ideas.

As Figure 3-2 shows, the three examples discussed fall in different parts of the quadrant. Malcom-Piqueux identified the Morrill Land Grant Acts as race-conscious policies designed to exclude members of racially minoritized groups. She identified the G.I. Bill as a race-neutral policy designed to include more members of those groups, but noted that it was compromised

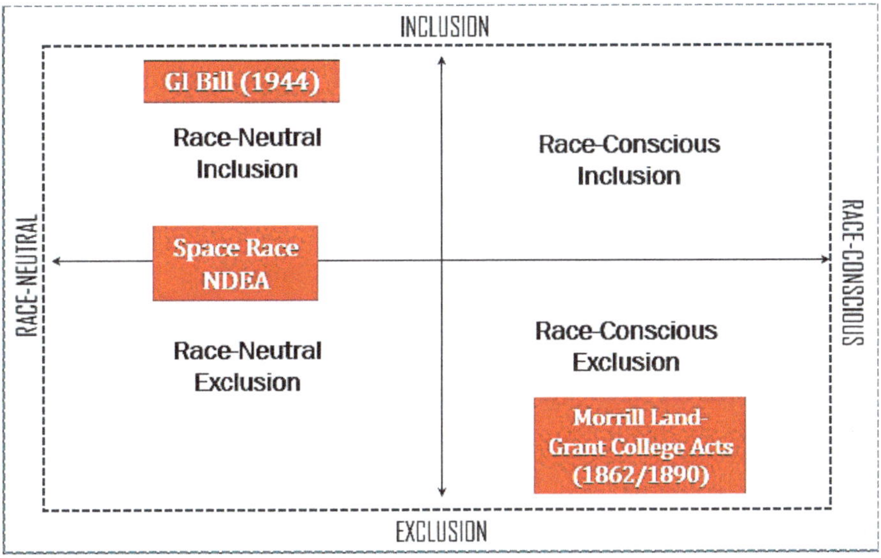

FIGURE 3-2 Equity quadrant framework for understanding race in higher education policies. SOURCE: Adapted from Malcom-Piqueux Symposium slides.

by a lack of attention to obstacles that would prevent an equitable distribution of the benefits. She classified the NDEA as race-neutral in that it also did not take racial attitudes into account and had both inclusionary and exclusionary effects.

LEARNING FROM THE PRESENT

Malcom-Piqueux closed with some broader reflections on considering racial equity and higher education. She pointed out that for the historical examples cited, there was generally no explicit discussion at the time of how the changes would impact racial equity. In order to improve equity in the future, though, the higher education community must have these conversations. She therefore offered some lessons to be learned from institutions that are currently advancing racial equity in STEM fields by making racial equity a central goal in their policies, particularly Minority-Serving Institutions (MSIs) and Community Colleges. "Those institutions that are successful at creating equitable conditions in relation to STEM as well as in relation to education more broadly have made it a mission to ensure that all students and racially minoritized students in particular are served well, and the cultures are supportive of these students," she observed.

Dealing directly with race is essential, Malcom-Piqueux went on, because race-specific problems cannot be solved with race-neutral solutions. Institutions are most likely to effectively address the problems when they identify racial equity as a primary indicator of their success. She described some key elements of the systemic approach to race-conscious inclusion she regards as necessary. It is critical to ensure that students from racially minoritized groups understand the relevance of STEM to their lives and their careers, she noted, and incorporating a wide range of pedagogical and instructional approaches is one strategy for doing that.

Race-conscious inclusion also requires that faculty members, administrators, and staff recognize and discard deficit-based thinking about inequities. A deficit model for understanding inequity is one in which the inequitable results experienced by a disadvantaged group are attributed to perceived deficits within that community, without any attention to the historic denial of opportunity that created the inequities in the first place. Educators who reject the deficit model, Malcom-Piqueux explained, instead share responsibility for producing racial equity. They recognize that inequitable outcomes indicate that current practices are not working and need to be changed. Reconsidering the ways that STEM fields define merit and identify promising students is a key step. Reliance on standardized test scores, for example, has yielded inequitable results, she noted, whereas holistic reviews can better identify those with the potential to excel in STEM subjects.

Community Colleges and MSIs, including HBCUs, Hispanic-Serving Institutions (HSIs), and Asian American, Native American, and Pacific Islander-Serving Institutions (ANAPISIs), are demonstrating the possibilities for rectifying educational inequities, Malcom-Piqueux explained. The MSIs in particular use culturally responsive approaches to instruction and assessment to foster an inclusive environment. They also typically have diverse faculty members who are invested in serving the institutions' target populations.

Community Colleges also create multiple pathways to STEM careers and stress the importance and relevance of STEM to students' goals, careers, and lives. Community Colleges can respond nimbly to labor market needs, and many develop partnerships with 4-year institutions, local industry, and other organizations to craft beneficial educational experiences for their students. Malcom-Piqueux noted that for-profit institutions play a large role in the way Black Americans are accessing higher education. Acknowledging concerns about student financing for these programs and other reasons for caution, she commented that the most successful for-profit institutions have used flexible modes of instructions, including online instruction, to meet student needs.

In conclusion, Malcom-Piqueux argued that racial equity should be a primary measure of success in the transformation of the undergraduate

STEM education system. She called for thinking about racial equity as an imperative rather than merely a nice thing to have and said that "if we do not achieve racial equity, then that means we are not being successful and we need to change our behavior in order to achieve success. Rather than it being an afterthought, have it lead how we think about how we are going to approach undergraduate STEM education in the future." She pointed out that achieving systemic change requires targeting all aspects of undergraduate education from policy to institutions and schools to educators, as well as the surrounding context in which all of this is taking place, thus ensuring that we are targeting all aspects of the system rather than tinkering around the edges as has often been done up to now.

4

Learning from Today's Students

To inform thinking about the need for future changes, experts in education research were asked to share selected data from their work on undergraduate students (see Box 4-1). In particular, the speakers were asked to consider issues related to access, inclusion, equity, and outcomes for undergraduate STEM students with a variety of backgrounds and goals. The research was conducted at different types of institutions of higher education, including Community Colleges and Hispanic-Serving Institutions (HSIs). It focused on students of different racial, ethnic, cultural, and geographic backgrounds and included students sometimes referred to as "nontraditional" due to their age, their pathway into postsecondary learning, or the credential being pursued (certificates or associate's degrees in addition to baccalaureate degrees). The speakers noted the importance of keeping in mind that many undergraduates are not between 18 and 22 years old and that a large percentage of them attend Community Colleges, not 4-year institutions.

COMMUNITY COLLEGE TECHNICIAN EDUCATION

Tyson described findings from his research on Community College associate's degree and certificate programs for technicians conducted through a research collaboration (Targeted Research in Technician Education, or PathTech).[1] PathTech's research has examined pathways in technical

[1]Tyson based his presentation on work supported by the National Science Foundation under Grant No. 1501999. Additional information about PathTech LIFE and other PathTech projects is available at www.PathTechUSF.com (accessed October 8, 2021).

BOX 4-1
STEM Education for Whom?

What can we learn from data about equity, inclusion, and outcomes for current students and how can that inform future decisions?

Panelists:
William Tyson, Associate Professor of Sociology, University of South Florida
Anne Marie Núñez, Professor of Educational Studies, The Ohio State University
Erin Cech, Assistant Professor of Sociology, University of Michigan

Moderator:
Josipa Roksa, Director of Strategic Academic Programs and Professor of Sociology and Education, University of Virginia

education—programs that typically offer applied, hands-on learning designed to develop practical skills and prepare students for the workforce—using a national survey and longitudinal follow-up interviews. Advanced technology fields covered by such programs include engineering technology, energy and environmental technology, advanced manufacturing, microtechnology, and nanotechnology, Tyson explained. Because these programs provide skills and credentials for advancing careers or initiating entrepreneurial ventures, he noted, they are an alternative version of the "T" in STEM, which is different from the more theoretical technology education offered in baccalaureate degree programs. This alternative is important, he noted, because not everyone has the privilege of time to pursue a 4-year degree. The technical programs Tyson has studied allow individuals to cycle between full-time work in sub-baccalaureate jobs and full-time school.

In one study, PathTech Tampa Bay, Tyson and his colleagues conducted interviews with students, faculty, administrators, and employers in the Tampa Bay, FL, area to examine student pathways into four Community College engineering technology programs and from those programs into employment (Fletcher and Tyson, 2017a, 2017b; Smith, 2017). The students identified four motivations for entering engineering technology programs: learning, credentialing, re-skilling, and empowering.

The students who identified learning as their prime motivation, Tyson explained, had developed an interest in education through engineering technology. These students had high school diplomas or general education degrees and enjoyed working with their hands. They reported that the content of engineering technician classes were of great interest and had motivated them to pursue higher education, many for the first time.

The students who were focused on earning the credentials necessary to enter the technician workforce had completed high school, and many had some college credits. They described themselves as having been good students in the past, but few had been exposed to engineering technology through school or work. Most had a stable work history in a non-STEM field, Tyson noted, but wished to enter the technician workforce. Other students—those focused on re-skilling—hope to find better and more stable work. Many had established careers in manufacturing or related fields but had been laid off or were not advancing in their careers. The fourth group, those who sought empowerment, reported that they hoped to gain the respect of others and perhaps fulfill a lifelong dream of earning a degree in higher education. Overall, said Tyson, the interviews suggested that these programs had a transformative effect on the students by improving their short-term and long-term prospects.

An ongoing national survey, PathTech Life, has been documenting multiple characteristics of Community College students in advanced technology fields (Tyson et al., 2018). The researchers have developed a database of information about 3,216 students from 96 colleges that includes academic experience, employment, motivation to enroll, program evaluation, academic goals, career goals, and demographic background. Figures 4-1 and 4-2 show some of the data collected through PathTech Life.

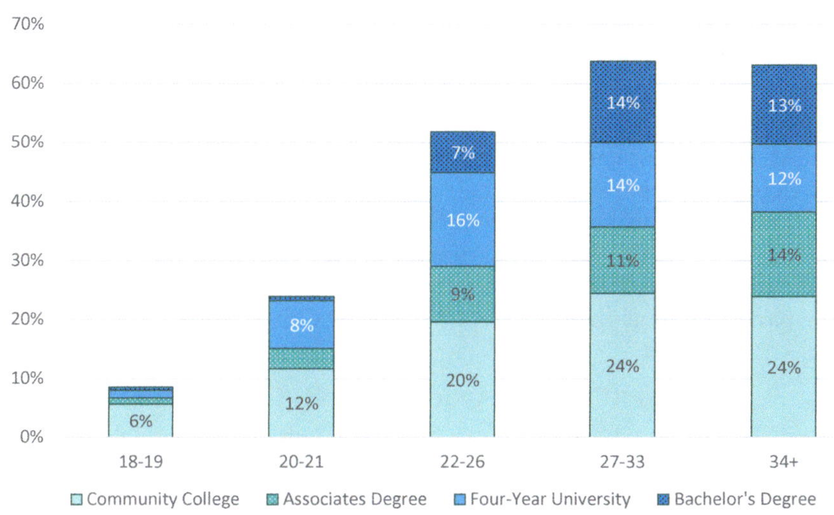

FIGURE 4-1 Prior enrollment and degree attainment for Community College students in advanced technology fields.
SOURCE: Tyson presentation.

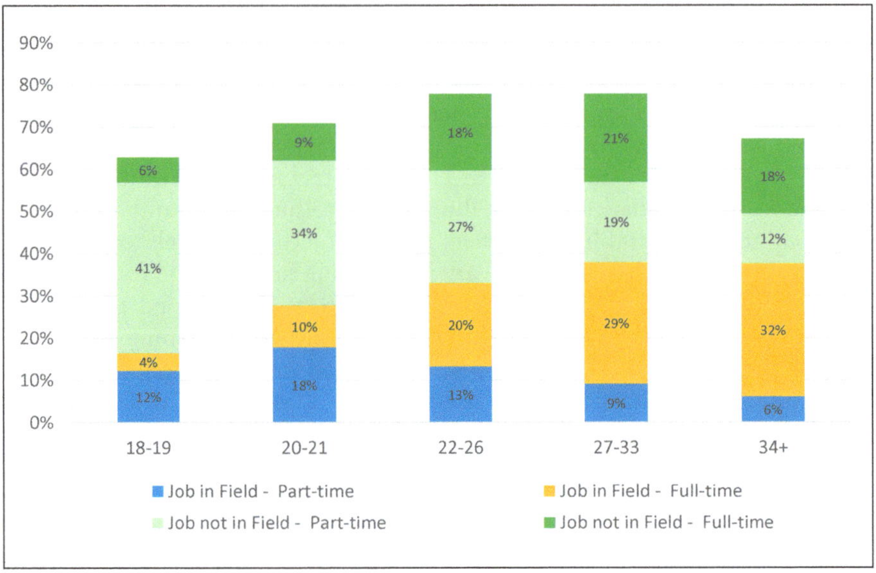

FIGURE 4-2 Employment status for Community College students in advanced technology fields.
SOURCE: Tyson presentation.

In a third project, PathTech Listen, researchers followed up on students who had participated in PathTech Life using interviews and a survey. A significant majority of the students were in jobs related to their field of study or had transferred to a 2- or 4-year institution to pursue further study in a STEM field. Most reported that their 2-year college programs provided them excellent preparation for their current jobs or school environment. A second set of interviews were devoted to understanding how the COVID-19 pandemic affected the students' careers, families, and personal lives. A third set of interviews will address the long-term goals and aspirations of the study participants as they navigate a post-COVID world.

LESSONS FROM HISPANIC-SERVING INSTITUTIONS

The implications of engaging undergraduate students in fieldwork and other student-centered approaches were the focus on Núñez's study of geoscience and computing at HSIs. She also looked at broader contributions of HSIs to the education of students from underresourced and minoritized backgrounds. Núñez noted that fieldwork seemed to open doors for students who may have believed they could not compete with students from more advantaged backgrounds. For many students, these experiences develop a sense of self-efficacy and confidence, she noted (Núñez et al., 2021).

Núñez's work is grounded in the multilevel intersectionality approach pioneered in Black feminist theory, which she applies in the context of STEM education (Núñez et al., 2020). One aspect of the intersectionality approach, she explained, is a focus on how a student's multiple identities may be fluid such that particular identities may be more salient in one setting than another. She noted, for example, that a disability that does not affect a student's capacity to engage in classroom activities could become salient during fieldwork. The approach also entails attention to institutional power domains that shape student experiences such as disparities in institutional resources and cultural and historical contexts that have influenced the disciplines students are engaging with. Geoscience, for example, has developed in the context of a history of colonization and extraction of resources by western powers (Sansone et al., 2019).

Núñez highlighted a National Academies report on Minority-Serving Institutions (MSIs) that highlighted strategies found to be effective at addressing the challenges many students from minoritized groups face (NASEM, 2020): (a) dynamic, multilevel, mission-driven leadership; (b) institutional responsiveness to meet students where they are; (c) supportive campus environments; (d) tailored academic and social supports; (e) mentorship and sponsorship; (f) undergraduate research experiences; and (g) "mutually beneficial" public- and private-sector partnerships.

She explained some lessons from her work on effective STEM strategies at HSIs conducted through the Computing Alliance of HSIs Network. This group, composed of more than 40 HSI department chairs, faculty, and staff who aim to raise Hispanic computing attainment, uses a variety of student-level supports such as research experiences and professional clubs (Villa et al., 2019). They also connect students with industry, engage students in peer-led learning, and take them to professional conferences in the discipline. Since 2000, this group has encouraged Hispanic students to pursue computing and increased their numbers in comparison with enrollment at institutions that do not use these strategies, Núñez observed.

Núñez closed with her thoughts about how STEM educators can continue to build the equity of STEM programs. Effective strategies, in her view, address the climate at the academic department level but also across the institution and within the discipline as a whole. At each of these levels, she added, equity requires attention to the salience of students' multiple identities with respect to learning contexts. She called on educators to learn from what HSIs and MSIs have accomplished and not rely solely on studies conducted at well-resourced, historically White institutions that are not representative of students or institutions across the United States.

CULTURAL MECHANISMS OF UNDERREPRESENTATION AND INEQUALITY

How do seemingly benign and objective cultural beliefs and practices perpetuate inequality both within the professional context of STEM and beyond? Cech identified this as the central question that can explain persistent underrepresentation for certain groups and inequality. "The way we think about what defines STEM and who defines what belongs and who belongs in STEM are vital for understanding how processes of inequality are perpetuated," she observed.

When institutions develop processes for admitting students or hiring or promoting faculty, she explained, they have established ways of measuring excellence and competence, which she called cultural yardsticks. Cech's sociology research has shown that these cultural yardsticks are often warped by biases and do not necessarily identify the characteristics that are actually required for success in STEM (Cech and Blair-Loy, 2021; Cech et al., 2018a). STEM leaders typically define scientific excellence in terms of abilities such as mathematical prowess and capacity for logical reasoning, but success in STEM fields also requires other capacities such as communication skills and the ability to provide mentoring or manage a lab, Cech observed. "By taking cultural yardsticks seriously as cultural constructs, we begin to see how these things are gendered, rationalized, and heteronormative." Her study of women in engineering majors, for example, has shown that they are less likely to remain in engineering departments when they perceive a disconnect between their own attributes and those that are valued in the field (Cech et al., 2011).

Cech found that cultural beliefs in STEM fields have a profound influence in other ways. She used the phrase "Euro-Western epistemologies" to describe the cultural rules that govern key aspects of STEM fields, which can have the effect of marginalizing and excluding some students. Decisions about what can and should be studied, how problems should be defined, and even what scientific endeavors should be funded, she explained, are cultural and social decisions. Native American students who have grown up with different epistemologies used for centuries in their cultures may, for example, experience what she described as delegitimization and erasure of those Indigenous ways of knowing when they enter the world of undergraduate STEM education (Cech et al., 2017; Cech et al., 2018b). When Native American students later decide to work in tribal communities, she noted, they often experience tension related to the disconnect and pressure to conform to Western approaches or epistemological imperialism.

In Cech's view, addressing cultural beliefs about what counts as legitimate thinking in a STEM context is the path forward rather than attempting to ignore these influences. One response to the issues that have been raised is depoliticization, she explained, a commitment to the idea that STEM is a pure domain that can be stripped of cultural and political concerns. This view, Cech said, considers inequality and social justice as political and cultural concerns that are either "irrelevant to true or pure STEM work or even potentially dangerous to the objectivity and neutrality in STEM." Attempting to depoliticize STEM education, she argued, silences the voices of students who experience marginalization and devaluation (Cech et al., 2018a).

Successfully diversifying STEM, Cech concluded, is not simply a matter of increasing the numerical representation of groups who have been underrepresented. In her view, true diversification requires an alteration of deeply held cultural beliefs about who counts as competent and excellent and what counts as valuable STEM work.

DISCUSSION

Following the presentations about their scholarly work, a discussion focused on the presenters' views about the highest priority changes needed in undergraduate STEM education. For Tyson, the most important priority is to begin understanding pathways to STEM education and moving away from the pipeline model in which it is assumed that all students follow similar trajectories through school and into a career. "People are cycling through different jobs, different educational experiences, and different life experiences, and they are doing so at different times," Tyson noted. In his view, a more inclusive model would incorporate different ways of living and different cultural models for adapting to the challenges of life and schooling.

Núñez emphasized the importance of understanding who today's students are and meeting them where they are. That understanding will be the foundation for developing more interactive collaborative and experiential STEM learning opportunities, she noted, such as laboratory sessions scheduled in the evening rather than in the middle of the day. Cech cited the importance of expanding understanding of what STEM means, to move away from what she described as corporate notions of advancement in science. In her view, STEM learning should be aimed at developing the expertise, perspectives, and skills needed to address issues important to society.

Various participant questions led to additional comments from Cech in which she elaborated on her point regarding cultural beliefs. She explained that there are multiple ways to think about what the role of STEM fields should be in society and how these fields make contributions. She expressed concern that what is seen as integral to problem-solving in STEM and what is seen as irrelevant "are completely arbitrary and are culturally determined and defined." Specifically, Cech expressed the hope that universities will move beyond what she called "the cultural permissibility of ignorance" to a place that values the issues and experiences of Indigenous populations.

A few participants also asked about how collaboration between 2-year and 4-year institutions can support the development of students with an array of backgrounds and needs. Tyson noted that many students, and even many programs, do not fit traditional performance measures that can be tied to state funding requirements. A student may take a course to acquire the skills needed for a promotion at work, for example, but if they do not complete degree requirements or matriculate full time, a state might consider that student a dropout. "Four-year institutions need to be more open to different ways people move back and forth between 2-year and 4-year institutions," said Tyson. He also called for 4-year institutions to offer more credentialing programs that do not require 4 years to complete.

Núñez responded to a question about opportunities for rural students to gain exposure to STEM professions with ideas such as outreach by alumni associations. She noted that opportunities in disciplines that are rarely taught at the K–12 level such as geoscience and computer science are especially important for students from minority groups. Tyson agreed that rural students are at a disadvantage in terms of exposure to STEM fields, and that educators may be unduly influenced by the fact that in many rural areas, there are very few STEM jobs. He suggested that efforts are needed at the county, state, and federal levels to boost opportunities for STEM-related entrepreneurship in rural areas.

Planning committee member and University of Virginia faculty member Josipa Roksa summed up the panel discussion by highlighting all that research-oriented universities and elite institutions can learn from open-access institutions, MSIs, HSIs, and HBCUs regarding aspirations for STEM education if they "think about structure and culture together." She added that "good things will not happen just because we wish to have a more diverse world in 2040," she said. That sort of change will require "intentional, day-to-day, month-to-month, year-to-year activities that we all have to engage in."

5

Designing for Tomorrow's Students: Creating Equitable Opportunities for Undergraduate STEM Students

In advance of the symposium, an idea competition was held to ask for input from the community on what undergraduate STEM education should look like in 2040. Entries into the competition were shared with participants to spark discussions at the symposium about how to explicitly and intentionally design learning experiences that create equitable opportunities for future students. Inspired by the idea competition entries, multiple presenters in two different panels (see Boxes 5-1 and 5-2) reflected on their own experiences as students (including the challenges of being the first generation in their families to attend college), noted the important role Community Colleges play in providing access to undergraduate education, discussed the challenges of navigating education as a low-income person, explored how some students must defy the beliefs others have that a person of color does not belong in STEM, and called for increased access to relevant experiential learning.

IDEAS FOR 2040

Vicente Talanquer, university distinguished professor of chemistry at the University of Arizona, contributed to the panel discussion by elevating points made by idea competition winners about where STEM education should be by 2040. "I share the competition winners' vision of a future characterized by inclusive and equitable educational environments that create flexible and responsive learning opportunities for all types of students," he said. "We just need to figure out how to get there successfully." He noted that the idea competition winners are imagining a time where internal walls

BOX 5-1
Changing Landscapes: 2040 versus 2020

How could the structures, priorities, and approaches of higher education change by 2040?

Panelists:
Vicki Chandler, Provost and Chief Academic Officer, Minerva Schools at the Keck Graduate Institute
Mark Mitsui, President, Portland Community College
Tonya Matthews, Director of STEM Learning Innovation and Associate Provost for Inclusive Workforce Development, Wayne State University
Vincente Talanquer, University Distinguished Professor of Chemistry, University of Arizona
Lindsey-Malcom-Piqueux, Senior Institutional Research Analyst, Caltech

Moderator:
Annette Parker, President, South Central College; Committee Co-chair

BOX 5-2
Access and Inclusion: Beginning with the End in Mind

How could we design STEM learning experiences to increase access, create equity, and leverage community connections?

Panelists:
Theresa Maldonado, Vice President for Research and Innovation, University of California System
Yves Salomon-Fernández, President, Greenfield Community College
Shanika Hope, Principal Amazon Future Engineer, Amazon
Monica Van, Student, University of California, San Diego

Moderator:
Barbara Schaal, Mary Dell Chilton Distinguished Professor at Washington University in St. Louis; Committee Co-chair

between academic units are torn down to allow for integrative and interdisciplinary curricular paths and where external walls have disappeared to allow for relevant and contextualized learning that takes place through experiences in the community (see Boxes 5-3 and Box 5-4 for some excerpts from two winning idea competition entries).

BOX 5-3
Snapshot 1 from the Idea Competition

Putting Equity at the Front: A Choose-Your-Own-Adventure Approach to Engineering Education

Engineering is a pathway to a stable career with direct employabilty after earning an undergraduate degree, and yet it is perhaps the most rigidly structured, and consequently, this excludes STEM majors. If we put equity at the forefront, we could eliminate the hurdles to entering and pursuing engineering degrees that are based on privilege-laden K–12 education systems and long-standing university structures. If we put equity at the forefront, we would meet incoming students where they are, focus on asset-based approaches to engineering education, and focus on students as humans rather than commodities to be produced by a system that has failed many engineering learners for over a century. While there are multiple ways to accomplish an equity-first approach, we will use the notion "choosing your own adventure" in engineering education to illustrate a potential process to design changes based on an equity and social justice mindset from the start. In a choose-your-own-adventure book, there are multiple endings and multiple ways to get from a start to an end. Essentially, the proposed approach of a choose-your-own-adventure program is the opposite of current engineering education curricula, which have strict entry expectations and with tightly bound, nearly singular course completion pathways accompanied by rigid prerequisites and corequisites. The high credit requirements, narrow focus, and structural rigidity of engineering curricula are highly problematic from an equity perspective and are not student-focused. Offering courses once per year promotes fiscal efficiency within the university, for example, fewer instructors are needed when fewer courses are offered, rather than supporting student needs. If an equity perspective was adopted, courses would not only be restructured, but also be offered when the students need them, such that "getting out of sequence" and consequently losing time would not be an issue for students. To design a program from an equity perspective, we should ask a number of questions. What purpose does rigidity serve in engineering education? Why can students not choose what courses to take while considering their own background, knowledge, and skills without being penalized in time and money toward degree completion?

SOURCE: Holly Matusovich and Kai Jun Chew, Virginia Tech.

Matthews, the director of STEM learning innovation and associate vice provost for inclusive workforce development at Wayne State University, reflected on the idea competition entries and noted that many programs and interventions will need to be targeted to the needs of particular groups to be most effective, and she stressed the importance of including students in the development phase for that reason. Specifically, Matthews commented on the idea competition entry that proposed limiting or eliminating the use

BOX 5-4
Snapshot 2 from the Idea Competition

CampusXR: Where Real and Virtual Education Blends

In 2040, Campus XR will deliver a blended learning environment for undergraduate STEM education that seamlessly couples real and virtual environments. Campus XR blurs the line between the real and the virtual worlds by developing novel virtual spaces that are intimately connected to augmented real spaces. Actions in the virtual world such as drawing on a whiteboard will be reflected in the real world and vice versa. Our presence within Campus XR, whether in-person or virtually, will form a continuum between our virtual and physical embodiment, impacting how we interact, communicate, and collaborate on real and virtual worlds. Campus XR aims to be technology-agnostic, adaptive, and able to leverage new emerging technological means that students, instructors, and institutions could use now and in the future, such means as holographic projections and live omnidirectional images. Campus XR is grounded on existing concepts and technologies that need to be further developed and implemented. These technologies involve advancements in areas like the Internet of things, ubiquitous computing, and virtual reality, among many others. Perhaps more challenging is developing strategies and technologies that computationally mediate remote human presence in the physical environment. This can involve advancements in areas such as tangible interfaces, augmented reality, and holographic representations. Our vision therefore implies that a multidisciplinary approach involving efforts from several academic areas of expertise would be pursued.

SOURCE: Ricardo Eiris, Michigan Technological University; and Alexandre Gomes de Siqueira, Masoud Gheisari, and Benjamin Lok, University of Florida.

of exams in engineering education. She noted that this idea became less radical during the COVID-19 pandemic when many institutions moved to a pass-fail grading system. The disadvantage, she commented, is that students graduating without a grade point average could be disadvantaged when seeking admission to graduate school or looking for a job. Other ways to assess students' experiences, talents, and abilities will need to be devised before STEM educators eliminate exams and grading.

PERSONAL EXPERIENCES NAVIGATING EDUCATION

Multiple panelists shared aspects of their own experiences in STEM education. Salomon-Fernández, president of Greenfield Community College, shared her personal background as context for her reflections. She emigrated to the United States with her family when she was 12 years old, she told the group, and grew up in an impoverished, high-crime Boston neighborhood. She was told that she would never succeed in science or mathematics and thus now considers herself a statistical anomaly because she was able to accomplish that goal. She is committed to improving STEM education for women, people of color, and people from other marginalized or minoritized groups because she hopes to create more statistical anomalies like herself. Like Salomon-Fernández, Hope also considers herself an anomaly, and she partly credits a teacher who intervened in her early life as a student for her success at Amazon as a principal Amazon future engineer. Chandler, provost and chief academic officer at the Minerva Schools of the Keck Graduate Institute, highlighted the life-changing opportunities that Community Colleges offer, particularly for students from lower-income groups, citing the benefits that she as a low-income single mother without a high school degree derived from enrolling. "My local Community College offered me, a first-generation college student, a low-cost pathway to college that would have been impossible any other way," she commented. The experience allowed her to qualify for scholarships and transfer to University of California, Berkeley. Matthews noted that when she says that she is a product of affirmative action, people do not assume that she was a valedictorian, that she scored a 1500 out of 1600 points on the SAT, or that she went to upper-tier, predominantly White universities for both undergraduate and graduate school. She stated that "the assumption is that I was an unprepared student given an additional leg up and supported by a series of committed faculty and programs, etc., etc. And every time I walk into a room for a certain level, I have to have those conversations. The former is actually what is true."

DESIGNING FOR INCLUSION

Van called for STEM education to focus on and incorporate the values of today's students and future generations of students. "We need higher education with a higher purpose," she argued. In her view, STEM education experiences direct students' attention to their careers. "Why do we have to wait until we graduate to feel a sense of worth and belonging in the world?" she asked. Empowering students, Van states from her perspective as an undergraduate, requires centering undergraduate education around problem definition and not necessarily problem solving, given that the diagnosis of a problem is what determines possible solutions. Van added that "the students with the most challenges know their challenges best, so they should be included in the critique of society, the reframing of what work needs to be done to adequately understand where the current society is failing them and their future." In her opinion, empowering those students who face the biggest challenges is the only way to truly design for inclusion and equity, for these are the students who are living the problems that need solving. "When you place the focus of education on evaluating how well students solve problems, we automatically disadvantage those with fewer resources to do the solving, but if we pivot education to how well students discover and articulate problems that would be worth their while to understand and solve for themselves, then we give those with the most problems the microphone," said Van. She then noted the importance of giving students a clear understanding of how complex the world is, and that complexity implies that there is no one right answer to the problems confronting education.

Maldonado noted that the current student body is the most diverse generation ever (Selingo, 2018). In California, where she serves as vice president for research and innovation for the University of California system, for example, she noted, 42 percent of all undergraduates are Hispanic. This generation of students has also been shaped by the great recession of 2008 and more recently by the COVID-19 pandemic and its economic consequences in that they are very worried about financial security, she emphasized. For this reason, she suggested, they view college differently than previous generations may have. "They seek relevance in their education for employment, and they favor student support over fancy amenities," she said. Some 42 percent of this generation of students expect to work for themselves, she added.

In her view, the STEM community needs to stop treating STEM and the arts and humanities as mutually exclusive and to stop talking about STEM in the aggregate. In addition, the STEM community needs to think about how to talk about STEM literacy for the population as a whole, not just for STEM majors. One important trend she has heard from industry is that within 10 years, 100 percent of jobs will be affected by artificial intelligence, so every student must be ready for that. "Our degree programs are so structured that I think we are losing sight of our ability to innovate and to be entrepreneurial, which are very important mindsets if you start your own company or if you work for a big company," said Maldonado.

Planning committee co-chair and Washington University in St. Louis faculty member Barbara Schaal asked Maldonado how the future demographic tsunami that will wash over the United States will affect university procedures and processes such as recruitment, admissions, student services, and all of the supports needed for a diverse student body. Maldonado, speaking specifically about Hispanics, said the number of Hispanic-Serving Institutions (HSIs) is growing. California, for example, has 170 HSIs, while 5 of the 10 University of California campuses are HSIs. The question is whether higher education structures are adapting to today's students. Approximately half of all engineering faculty come from other countries, while the undergraduate population is primarily domestic, creating a disconnect. There is also the matter of implicit bias (NASEM, 2018a, 2020) and sexual harassment (NASEM, 2018b) that drives students away from STEM. "When we are ready to be honest about our climate issues and recognize the demographics—who is in our undergraduate programs and who is coming in the future—the institutions themselves and the faculty and the staff need to really look and be ready and adapt to the students who are coming," said Maldonado.

Hope, the Amazon engineer, explained that given the speed at which technology is advancing, the way institutions train and support the workforce has to be more flexible and more of an ecosystem or network of learning that creates cycles of learning and earning throughout life. Speaking about college degrees and other credentials including nanodegrees, Hope said they "all have to work as a collective to enable this idea of lifelong learning and the ability to acquire new skills as jobs and labor markets change and evolve." She added that the notion that a baccalaureate degree and credentials are in competition is wrong. Instead, they have to work together to create additional avenues for learners to upskill and reskill and to serve as on- and off-ramps in the learning journey.

Hope explained that the work she leads in her job at Amazon is to promote equitable access to STEM for students from underrepresented groups in the technology sector, including Indigenous and rural students. She focused on the skills needed for future success in the workforce, citing findings in a recent report from the World Economic Forum. The report identified the skills most in demand across all job categories are critical thinking and analysis, problem-solving, and self-management, which include active learning, resilience, stress tolerance, flexibility, and adaptability (WEF, 2020). Employers surveyed for the report see significant gaps in the current workforce, Hope added. They estimate that 40 percent of current workers and new hires require at least 6 months of development to acquire the skills needed to ensure they remain relevant and that their companies continue to be competitive. At Amazon, Hope explained, managers describe the development employees need to thrive as requiring a "learn and be curious" mindset or lifelong learning. Reflecting on what should be expected of undergraduate STEM students in 2040, Hope suggested that they will need to "embody the tried-and-true four Cs: curiosity, critical thinking, communication, and collaboration." These four skills are the foundation that will allow them to pivot and adapt in a constantly evolving labor market.

Salomon-Fernández noted that higher education today is preparing students for jobs that do not exist. "We need to understand that what prospective employers and incumbent workers, professionals and non-professionals will need is education that does not translate into a degree," she said. "They are not going to need four master's degrees or a Ph.D. for these jobs. What they need is lifelong learning and continuing education." Salomon-Fernández answered a participant's question about her mention of transdisciplinarity, sharing her thoughts on why it has great potential for increasing access, equity, and inclusion in STEM fields. Salomon-Fernández first explained that when she talks about transdisciplinarity, she is referring to education that goes beyond interdisciplinarity and multidisciplinarity and is rooted deeply in connections with the community. What that implies, she said, is the need to connect experiential learning opportunities with the communities in which students live so that learning becomes rooted in the real world rather than remains abstract and conceptual. This approach, she noted, fits the desires of today's students to apply their education to tackle the problems confronting their communities, the nation, and the planet. Van, in agreeing with Salomon-Fernández, said that students very much want purpose in their education.

Schaal asked the panelists to identify one important concept they feel is important given their individual perspectives. Maldonado replied that the culture within the university has to change regarding equity and sexual harassment, which points to the need for faculty, staff, and administrator development and training to be more sensitized to these issues and understand them better. Salomon-Fernández said that mentors, representation, and role models matter, particularly for first-generation students from marginalized and minoritized populations. She noted that most U.S. students can go from kindergarten to a Ph.D. and never have a Black female educator in their lives. "We need more faculty who represent nondominant groups, and that definition varies based on the discipline," said Salomon-Fernández. "We need to have folks from the dominant groups to act not only as mentors but as sponsors for the groups that are traditionally not represented. We need people to stick their necks out because marginalized people are not going to bust open those doors themselves. What we need are allies who are committed to this work and people who have reached the pinnacle of their career or are near it who can say they support equity and that they want to help this next generation because it is the right thing to do."

Hope, the Amazon engineer, agreed with her colleagues and stressed that achieving equity will take a village. "This is a shared responsibility as we think about reimagining how we equip and educate tomorrow's sets of leaders and tomorrow's workforce," said Hope. She also pointed to the importance of recognizing the value of work-based learning and of listening to the voice of students and giving them a choice about how they move through their educational experience. Van, the undergraduate student, added that higher education needs to better recognize the value of human potential to develop and contribute.

Schaal said that what has come across to her is the idea that education does not give the student much subject-specific value and expertise. Instead, it gives them fundamental tools or virtues that will enable them to continue their education throughout their lives. She also noted the need to disrupt the current educational system and the expectations people have for the educational system so that students develop into more well-rounded individuals.

Chemistry professor Talanquer reflected on the paper by Malcom-Piqueux (see Chapter 3 for a discussion of the paper on Transformation in the U.S. Higher Education System: Implications for Racial Equity) and agreed that achieving this imagined future will require major and sustained changes in the traditional structures, policies, and practices that have failed to serve many students. Such change cannot occur without engagement in deliberate and intentional action by all stakeholders, he added. Higher education faculty will need to change the way they think about curricular design, teaching, and assessment of student learning, he observed. Redesigning the introductory courses in STEM departments that so frequently hinder the advancement of capable STEM students, for example, would make an important difference. Similarly, many STEM curricula are designed as a series of isolated courses, but alternate curriculum designs would better prepare students for active participation in multidisciplinary projects driven by socially acute questions. Additionally, assessments that measure student growth rather than knowledge acquisition can better foster a student's ownership and agency in their own learning.

These types of changes, Talanquer suggested, move beyond what he described as peripheral efforts to change the instruction offered by individual faculty members and instead adopt models that demand multiunit engagement in "critical action projects that have demonstrable impacts on the achievement, persistence, and retention of minority students." This is most important in large public universities, he added, where the focus on research productivity is traditionally used as an excuse for the lack of meaningful transformation.

Matthews called for attention to equity and for "specific language around Black students, African American students, Latinx students, and immigrant students." She noted the need for intentionality about the voices at the table and mentioned a favorite phrase of hers: "do nothing about me without me." Harkening back to her training as an engineer, she called for treating the need to bring new voices to the table as a systems engineering problem that can be solved with a focused effort. In addition, she called for supporting faculty in the challenging task of offering more project-based learning in order to prepare students for career and research. She noted the need to incentivize this way of teaching and to support faculty in making changes.

One way for 4-year institutions to pursue these sorts of changes, Chandler noted, is to reward teachers for improving their practice to advance equity. While multiple-choice exams are very simple to grade, she said that making the transition to project- and problem-based assignments that allow students to demonstrate what they have learned and build strong portfolios takes much more effort on the faculty member's part. Matthews and Talanquer agreed, noting the importance of changing our concept of how faculty work, questioning and reevaluating the way teaching is approached as an individual isolated task, considering education as a collective responsibility, and considering ways to promote collaboration between educators.

A CRUCIAL ROLE FOR COMMUNITY COLLEGES

Portland Community College president Mitsui emphasized that while talent is universal, opportunity is not, and that Community Colleges are designed to make opportunity universal. These institutions have democratized education in the United States, he noted, by offering open access while also facilitating the process of transferring to institutions that award baccalaureate degrees. A newer focus, he observed, is to strive for not only equitable access but also equitable student success. The asset-based approach mentioned by Malcom-Piqueux is one key, Mitsui noted, but analysis of both qualitative and quantitative data is needed to support strategies for reducing disparities. Narrowing the $78 billion funding gap between Community Colleges and universities, would also help, he added.

Demographic changes in the United States are likely to make the role of Community Colleges even more important, Matsui noted. By 2030, immigration will account for a larger component of U.S. population growth than natural increase (births), and Community Colleges are a key avenue by which new immigrants become integrated into U.S. society.[1] In many Community Colleges, language acquisition is embedded in the education and training Community Colleges offer and contextualized within career pathways. This is "an effective way for students to gain upward economic mobility," he explained. In his view, culturally and linguistically relevant, technology-enhanced instruction with qualified faculty can contribute to an expanded and more diverse STEM workforce that is both bilingual and bicultural.

Income inequality and associated challenges related to food, housing, and income insecurity are significant issues for two-thirds of Community College students, Matsui went on. Creative thinking is needed to address these problems if higher education is to meet goals for inclusion by 2040. Providing support services and funding to address these basic needs could be automated, he suggested. He noted that the Internal Revenue Service already collects most of the information needed for means-tested benefits.

---

[1]See https://www.census.gov/content/dam/Census/library/publications/2020/demo/p25-1144.pdf.

This system could be the foundation for other uses, such as determining eligibility for Pell grants, food stamps, section 8 housing, and other supports.

Chandler observed that Community Colleges and Minority-Serving Institutions (MSIs) have adopted practices that all institutions of higher education can learn and scale to accelerate needed changes, and agreed with the concept developed in a paper submitted to the idea competition ("Improving Diversity in STEM through Community College Partner Programs" by Kathryn McGill[2]) that expanding partnerships between Community Colleges and 4-year institutions is a good pathway for improving diversity in STEM. "But facilitating transfer will not be sufficient," Chandler went on to say. "Institutions must incorporate cultural assessment and other kinds of practices from Community Colleges and MSIs to support those students' successes." If the higher education community is to meet the National Science Board's goal of bringing the "missing millions" into STEM, she noted, institutions need to move immediately to welcome and include all students and implement and scale proven practices (National Science Board, 2020, 17). Achieving the goal of having the STEM workforce represent America's demographics by 2040, she added, will mean twice the current numbers of female and African-American workers in STEM fields and three times the number of Hispanic/Latinx workers. Accomplishing that will entail unprecedented changes and cooperation across the STEM education ecosystem.

---

[2]Video is available at https://www.nationalacademies.org/event/10-21-2020/imagining-the-future-of-undergraduate-stem-education-symposium.

6

The Role of Technology

The role of technology in educational experiences and ethical issues presented by rapidly evolving technological developments were the focus of a panel discussion. Panelists were asked to explore the complex issues raised by current and potential technological developments, the ways in which individuals and society can make informed decisions about technology's use, and ways in which undergraduate STEM students can be helped to consider these issues throughout their education (see Box 6-1). Panelists were selected to provide perspectives from industry, government, and academia.

Michael Torrence of Motlow State Community College opened the panel discussion by explaining how he and colleagues are applying a concept they call TILT (teaching, innovation, learning, and training) to STEM education. They chose to use this approach in an attempt to increase the percentage of Tennesseans with postsecondary degrees or certifications to 55 percent by 2025. TILT is targeted at people who are between jobs or seeking new skills at a Community College. His institution also focuses on technology as a core component of students' ability to become entrepreneurs, and sees entrepreneurship as particularly helpful to those from the state's rural areas who want a good career but who do not want to leave their rural communities.

Schatz explained that the initiative she heads, Advanced Distributed Learning (ADL), aims to modernize the way the United States and its international partners conduct digital and online training and education. ADL is a federal program housed under the Defense Human Resources Agency that serves the federal workforce and partners in industry and academia.

BOX 6-1
Fast-Changing Technology: Uses and Ethical Issues

What are the key issues to consider in terms of how technology can alter educational experiences?

Panelists:
Michael Torrence, President, Motlow State Community College
Sae Schatz, Director, Advanced Distributed Learning, U.S. Department of Defense
Nishal Mohan, Founder, mohuman
Nicole Jackson, Chief Technology Officer, Duet Health

Moderator:
Leanne Chukoskie, Director, Power of NeuroGaming (PoNG) Center, University of California, San Diego, committee member

It aims to demonstrate the use of diverse kinds of technology to provide high-quality education, training, and informal learning.[1] To achieve those goals ADL considers lessons from pedagogy, adult education, and other instructional approaches as important program components along with the technological tools.

In 2019, Schatz and her ADL colleagues worked with more than 85 professionals across industry, academia, K–12 education, government, and nonprofit organizations to identify what the future of learning, broadly defined, will look like. The resulting learning ecosystem developed from this effort leverages technology to create ubiquitous learning that blends all training and educational experiences and is driven by data. Data, said Schatz, makes learning experiences personalized and manageable, whether those experiences include training, education, workforce development, or informal learning. For this ecosystem to come to fruition, she explained, it will require new instructional techniques, challenges to governance and other types of policies, and an opening of the education aperture wide enough to admit the formal to informal learning spectrum and the individual to organizational/collective learning spectrum.

Mohan, whose nonprofit helps underserved people access digital services that improve their lives, predicted that the next 5 years will be exciting as the business models, public policies, and affordability of Internet services, as well as access to education, telemedicine, and other digital services become more democratized. He noted that students with access, updated

[1]Additional information is available at https://adlnet.gov/.

devices, and digital competency will have a clear advantage in the future workforce, which to him means that the education systems and supporting technologies need to be designed with the digitally underserved in mind, but they also need to be designed for use by everyone.

In the United States, some 42 million low-income and rural people do not have Internet access devices, software, or digital skills, said Mohan, and every day that situation leaves these Americans further behind in education, work, health care, and everyday life. "The COVID-19 pandemic conclusively showed that people who are not digitally prepared lose their education, their jobs, and even their lives because of digital inequities," said Mohan, "and while society becomes more dependent on these digitalized Internet-connected services and opportunities, digitally underserved students, individuals, and families are left out of the decision-making process and technology that decide their status in our society."

In her remarks, Jackson said that from her perspective in the health information industry, it is important to prepare students for jobs, but if STEM education does not want to suffer the same fate as home economics and shop classes in the K–12 environment, it is important to ensure that STEM remains relevant in American society, particularly in the lives of students who would benefit from a deep engagement in STEM. The way to start doing this, she said, is to "first start by understanding their interests and their needs and then leverage the data to let us know what they are actually interested in learning so that we can actually see transformational and traditional education have some form of fusion in the future."

Following the panelists remarks, planning committee member Leanne Chukoskie asked the panelists to discuss ideas on how to build the educational infrastructure in a way that incorporates digital technologies, physical attributes, and social and cultural issues in a way that is effective, inclusive, equitable, and resilient. Torrence replied that the place to start is ensuring that everyone has access to both Internet connectivity and the hardware needed to use that connectivity. Doing so would benefit all levels of education from K–12 through graduate school. He noted that there are actually few areas in the country that do not have fiber-optic cable available, making the challenge one of connecting all households. He said the nation should be ashamed if it does not make these connections now, given the rate at which technology is becoming an intimate part of educational and economic success.

Schatz said she could not agree more with Jackson's comments about the need for a fusion of traditional and transformational approaches, noting that the nation is on the cusp of having a learning ecosystem for the future. The technologies are available, she said, as are the different pathways of conveying knowledge and skills to those who need it most. There is also flexibility in terms of degrees, certificates, and microcredentials. Together, these tools, along with data, can create lifelong, highly personalized learning trajectories that have the potential to produce greater equity. The one possible downside has to do with an individual's data and who owns those data, the student or some company. Schatz said that if the issues of data privacy, interoperability, and sovereignty are resolved in a good way, the opportunities will exist to benefit all Americans. If done wrong, data could become an invisible shackle that people will struggle to understand, just as they do today with their social media data.

Jackson commented that the parallels between the issues confronting education and health information technology—the area in which she works—are "so profoundly shocking" that everyone needs to look at the path that health information technology has taken over the past 20 years in terms of influencing learners through social media and getting people of all ages and backgrounds familiar and more confident in technology. The Health Insurance Portability and Accountability Act provides lessons that could serve as a foundation for how education could deal with privacy and data ownership.

Mohan stressed the importance of working with communities, not in spite of them. As an example, he was part of a steering group to develop a digital inclusion roadmap for low-income neighborhoods. One of the ideas that came out of this group was to put charging stations for electric vehicles in those neighborhoods, even though few people in those neighborhoods have an electric car. He advocated for getting neighborhood leaders involved in the planning activities, and what those leaders told the steering group was that the biggest problem they had with technology was that high school students could not get jobs because they could not type given that they were all using iPads. "We need to work with the communities in looking at cultural problems that they are solving and co-develop solutions with them," said Mohan. Doing so will build trust and lead to higher rates of acceptance and adoption of technology, he added.

Reflecting on questions and comments made by symposium participants, Chukoskie noted the need to ensure that the use of technology in teaching is not implemented in ways that are detrimental to the identity of marginalized students. Related to that, she said there are dinosaurs in academia who are not necessarily thinking that way, and unfortunately, they comprise the majority of available educators in this generation. The question then becomes how academia can ensure that technology is lifting up marginalized students rather than keeping them in place. Jackson replied that the MIT Hackathon[2] does this very well by using decentralized mentoring from multidisciplinary subject matter experts from many different places. She believes that higher education should do the same. She also said

[2]Additional information is available at https://hackmit.org/.

that there is a process by which instructors are disseminating information and students are applying it, and if educators use culturally competent mentors to apply information, then it should be possible to do both well and create not only greater support for technology but also greater adoption of it.

Speaking of dinosaurs, Mohan said they are also making decisions on broadband investments, and those decisions have prioritized expanding broadband access in rural areas while largely ignoring urban areas that are underserved digitally and largely populated by Black and brown Americans. Torrence stressed the need to break down the silos that exist in academia so that academic affairs, student success, and workforce development are working together to benefit students. He also noted the importance of developing staff and administrators, not just faculty, as culturally competent individuals. Schatz added that providing broadband access is not the end of the process, given there is a big difference between having access to information and getting it through quality pedagogy with good mentors and access to structured, coherent, well-designed courses. "I worry that if we forget about those aspects, we will simply shift from having a lack of equity in access to now a lack of equity in the coherence of the information that is available," said Schatz.

Posing a question from a symposium participant, Chukoskie asked the panel to discuss the qualities of the future Internet. Mohan said the Federal Communications Commission defines broadband Internet as providing 25 megabits/second downloading and 3 megabits/second uploading, which he said is terrible. He proposed that 100 megabits/second in each direction should be standard so as to accommodate three people working or studying at home, all conducting Zoom meetings. He said that as he speaks to those who are designing the next generation of the Internet, he is seeing a lot of thought being pursued about ways to create an Internet that promotes student safety, curtails the spread of misinformation, and makes it easy to access good information and learn remotely. "It is hard to know exactly what can be done," said Mohan, "because there are so many regulations in place and influence from Internet service providers that is preventing progress." He also noted that the community broadband networks that are popping up across the country can have a big influence toward democratizing the Internet. Schatz commented that if the future Internet is designed correctly, it could create the possibility of having an "Internet of learning things" in which training and education technologies are able to communicate with one another thanks to interoperability.

7

Innovations and Strategies for Moving Forward

Strategies for pursuing the goals of STEM education were the focus of several discussions throughout the symposium. Anchored by Aikaterini Bagiati's presentation of a commissioned paper she wrote with Sanjay Sarma on Current Innovations in STEM Education and Equity Needs for the Future,[1] other presenters and participants considered new ways of thinking about curricula, approaches, and learning environments.

CURRENT INNOVATIONS IN STEM EDUCATION

Recent efforts to improve undergraduate STEM education and address inequities in the STEM environment were the focus of a paper prepared for the workshop by Sanjay Sarma and Aikaterini Bagiati and presented by Bagiati. The paper explored approaches to STEM education that the authors identified as innovative, transformative, and sustainable, and it examined ways in which these innovations supported institutional and societal goals for STEM education, including goals related to equity. The world now realizes that people need STEM education as much as STEM needs more people, said Bagiati. "We know that a quality STEM education can create better-informed citizens, people that are better able to navigate through the new digital and technology-oriented world and can create more opportunities for personal and professional development," said Bagiati, who noted that aside from needing more STEM professions to tackle

[1] A PDF of the paper can be found at https://www.nationalacademies.org/event/10-21-2020/imagining-the-future-of-undergraduate-stem-education-symposium.

many of society's challenges, STEM needs more professionals from diverse populations.

Bagiati explained that they grounded their analysis in common principles regarding equity in STEM education, including concepts of access, fairness, inclusion, and provision of opportunities for personalized learning and personal and social development. She noted that scholars and institutions who have focused on the pursuit of equity in STEM education have all moved beyond the goal of making STEM education more inclusive to considering ways to make it both structurally and culturally responsive, that is, to considering sources of bias and alienation that can repel students, as well as ensuring that language and interactions are relatable to students of diverse cultural backgrounds.

Bagiati described how the paper describes 10 pathways to innovation in STEM education (Table 7-1). She spoke at length on two of these pathways: applying active learning pedagogies and adopting a multidisciplinary/integrative approach to STEM education. Active learning pedagogies such as problem-based learning, task-based learning, and project-based learning have been discussed for decades. Over this period, active learning techniques have evolved from small-scale, hands-on activities to semester-long projects or even entire academic programs that place project-based learning techniques at the center of the academic experience. She argued that project-based and active learning could be used to advance an equity agenda by continuing to revise these techniques so that they increasingly reflect an approach that "calls for active student engagement with authentic, real-life problems and for projects deeply connected to student culture and identity." These approaches are designed to connect current learning experiences with

TABLE 7-1 Innovations in STEM Education

1. Applying active learning pedagogies	6. Enhancing inclusive entrepreneurship and innovation
2. Implementing competency based education	7. Providing advanced support mechanisms for educational research and development
3. Adopting a multidisciplinary/integrative approach	8. Developing new credentials
4. Supporting beyond classroom learning experiences	9. Support connections with K-12 and peer learning/mentoring
5. Providing flexible, cost efficient educational paths to continuous learning	10. Enhancing sharing and dissemination of information

SOURCE: Bagiati and Sarma commissioned paper, p. 5. https://www.nationalacademies.org/event/10-21-2020/imagining-the-future-of-undergraduate-stem-education-symposium.

the student's preexisting knowledge, allow for opportunities to engage in collaborative learning, allow for providing timely feedback, and foster growth at each student's own pace. The Community College Undergraduate Research Initiative (CCURI), Open Schools for Open Society (OSOS), and the Aalborg Center for Project Based Learning (PBL) were cited as projects and initiatives that incorporate best practices in active and project-based learning pedagogies.

It is clear, said Bagiati, that there are challenges to using active learning and inquiry-based approaches. Challenges arise particularly when the problem or project is poorly defined or adapted for instructional use, when there is insufficient guidance during the activity, or when the classroom scaffolding is inadequately designed. Additional effort might also be needed when learners are novices or when they are completely unfamiliar with the content of the method. "We need to reorient this approach and understand proper adaption and implementation," she said.

Regarding the move to multidisciplinary STEM education, she noted that there are now multidisciplinary programs at some institutions and even entire schools based on this idea. One trend that is encouraging to her is the incorporation of the humanities, arts, and social sciences into a multidisciplinary STEM curriculum. "We believe that a more human and equitable solution cannot arise unless citizens and professionals are also introduced to fundamental concepts and skills, deeply rooted to the fields of humanities, social sciences, and the liberal arts," Bagiati explained. As more schools adopt this approach, research will identify its strengths and weaknesses. So far, she noted, the full integration of humanities, arts, and social sciences into STEM curricula is challenging and overwhelming to faculty that do not have formal training in humanities, arts, and social science content. The Vertically Integrated Projects (VIP) program and the undergraduate curriculum of the (SUTD) are two organizations doing promising work in this realm.[2]

Bagiati said there are also other promising innovations for educational improvement:

- **Implementing competency-based education (CBE).** CBE approaches enable students to choose "from a wide range of learning experiences at school, online, and beyond and work with educators to build their own learning pathways." Southern New Hampshire University and Western Governors University were cited as pioneers working in CBE.[3]

[2]More information about VIP is available at https://www.vip.gatech.edu/vip-vertically-integrated-projects-program. More information about SUTD is available at https://www.sutd.edu.sg/Admissions/Undergraduate.

[3]More information about CBE is available at https://www.ed.gov/oii-news/competency-based-learning-or-personalized-learning.

- **Supporting learning experiences beyond the classroom.** Cocurricular experiences have benefits for student learning and development; however access to cocurricular involvement can raise issues of equity, as not all students have equal access to cocurricular opportunities due to financial constraints or other limitations to access.
- **Providing flexible, cost-efficient educational paths to continuous learning.** Changing student demographics and the growth of existing groups such as refugee students have led to the emergence of new credentials and other novel postsecondary educational opportunities. While platforms such as Coursera and edX have enabled much innovation in this area, equity concerns persist due to access limitations stemming from "the digital divide," as well as language and cultural barriers.

Bagiati said that the paper also presents a framework of strategies to build upon existing innovations as the field moves toward a more equitable vision of higher education in the STEM field. Suggested strategies were as follows:

- Careful design of content, assessment, and pedagogy (CAP) in STEM higher education
- Development of technology and infrastructure grounded in the science of learning
- Enhancement of teacher education and faculty development
- Implementation of new educational policies and strategies to support innovation
- Development of new national and global STEM credentials

To conclude her remarks, Bagiati said that progress has been made in terms of incorporating innovations into STEM education, but much opportunity remains, especially as the needs of the economy, insights into pedagogy, and emerging venues for education continue to evolve. "As we look toward the future, it is important to reflect on what has worked and what has not to ensure that this opportunity to reimagine STEM higher education yields ideas that encourage bold, sustainable solutions, not jury-rigged solutions based on convenience," said Bagiati. Moreover, she added, given that each innovation for the sake of improving education can either reduce various inequalities or exacerbate them if care is not taken with respect to design and implementation, it is important to ensure that the tide of innovation lifts all boats by way of equity-focused policies and practices at the institutional and state levels.

ALIGNING GOALS, STRUCTURES, AND STRATEGIES

Panelists were asked to reflect on how structures that currently shape undergraduate STEM education align with aspirations for the future and what strategies could help higher education achieve its goals in educating undergraduate STEM students (see Box 7-1). Panelists provided perspectives from a research university, a technical institute, a Community College, and those of a recent undergraduate.

In opening the panel, Mitra noted that the goals for undergraduate STEM education in 2040 are not materially different from the goals already being pursued: preparing students to tackle the complex societal problems of the twenty-first century. "I think it is for them to envision what has never been done and then do whatever it takes to make it happen," said Mitra. He also believes that postsecondary education should help students change who they are, expand their view of the world and their goals, and explore new ideas. One change he does want to see by 2040 is for there to be proper representation of all demographics in STEM, and the one thing he would expect undergraduates STEM students to learn in 2040 is to think more effectively. "Creative thinking, critical thinking, systems thinking, ethical thinking are tools that we will always find useful," said Mitra. He added that the pandemic has accelerated the need to adapt, be flexible,

BOX 7-1
Challenging Our Strategies and Expectations About Student Learning

Which educational structures best support STEM learning goals?

Panelists:
Amitava "Babi" Mitra, Ph.D., Executive Director, New Engineering Education Transformation (NEET), Massachusetts Institute of Technology
Suzanne Weekes, Associate Dean of Undergraduate Studies, Worcester Polytechnic Institute and Incoming Director, Society for Industrial and Applied Mathematics
Clarissa Sorensen-Unruh, Professor of Chemistry, Central New Mexico Community College
Sakereh Carter, Ph.D. Student, University of Maryland

Moderators:
Lynn Andrea Stein, Professor of Computer and Cognitive Science, Olin College, committee member
Monique Umphrey, President, Houston Community College, Northeast, committee member

and prepare for volatility, uncertainty, complexity, and ambiguity. It is no coincidence that all of these skills, he said, are those needed to work in a startup.

Today, said Mitra, education is more focused on content and skills and not so much on helping students learn how to learn and think more effectively. He commented that when students are motivated, they can do anything, which implies that teaching should be more relevant to students (understanding air quality versus learning quantum mechanics, for example).

Acknowledging that teaching engineering without quantum mechanics is sacrilegious with respect to standard engineering education, Mitra pointed out that today's technologies enable a student to enter the specifications for a car suspension part, for example, and have it produced in a matter of minutes. "You do not need any physical principles to do that," he said, "and given artificial intelligence and machine learning, we do not have to be engineers to design bolts and fasteners or a variety of other things."

In his opinion, it will be more useful for postsecondary education to produce generalists whose fundamentals are strong and who can use general-purpose tools such as calculus, artificial intelligence, computational tools, machine learning tools, and physical simulation and then apply those tools to solve important questions. "That is what I would like us to shoot for in 2040," said Mitra.

For Weekes, the most important goal of undergraduate STEM education should be to increase the understanding and awareness of what is going on in the world so that students will be better global citizens who can make ethical, sound decisions, and build healthier, safer, and more just societies. By 2040, she would like to see data incorporated naturally into education as a means of creating data-competent graduates and data-critical citizens. Along the same lines, she would like to see STEM education incorporate the social sciences, humanities, and arts to produce better-informed and critically thinking graduates who can communicate with the general public about what STEM means to society. What she would like to never hear again is a student ask, "When will I ever use this?" Finally, she would like to see STEM education produce STEM-competent people who will be at the table making policy decisions that affect everyone.

At her institution, Worchester Polytechnic Institute, every student has the opportunity to work on significant, open-ended problems as a requirement for graduation. That type of work, she said, helps students retain concepts and provides graduates with the satisfaction of already having worked on a real problem. She also noted that her school has built structures to welcome students who are from groups underrepresented in STEM and make them feel comfortable and appreciated in the STEM community. One of her passions, she said, has been connecting academia to industry to identify the problems industry is having and that students might attempt to solve.

Sorensen-Unruh said she believes in centering the humanity of students in any goal regarding STEM education, which to her is an issue of social justice. Doing so requires two actions: eliminating racism, misogyny, colonization and colonialism, homophobia and transphobia, and ableism among all STEM students, faculty, and administrators and treating all students with respect and compassion in a way that honors their lived experience. Creating a more equitable, diverse, inclusive, and socially just STEM education by 2040 should start with eliminating the "banking model" in content delivery and education. The banking model assumes that coursework deposits knowledge into students as if they were bank accounts. "As learning and cognitive scientists, we know knowledge is actively created and recreated by each student within their own learning process," she explained. To go along with that, there is a need to radically change class assessment and evaluation and incorporate strategies such as open-project or problem-based assessment. "Allowing our students to have an active role in their course evaluation, at least through a conversation with the instructor, is absolutely critical," said Sorensen-Unruh. "We must employ innovative solutions such as ungrading to enable students to recognize their own agency and power within their learning development in STEM, and until we change the conversation on how we assign grades, treating our students as humans will always be an afterthought." Sorensen-Unruh carries out her work with these goals at Central New Mexico Community College.

She also commented on the need to challenge all blind and unthoughtful use of educational technology, including what she called the predatory use of antiplagiarism software and artificial intelligence–powered exam proctoring software. A third step, she said, is to integrate digital and information literacy into course curricula and promote open access and open science so that all students can resource themselves appropriately today and in the future. The final step to creating a more equitable, diverse, inclusive, and socially just STEM education is to require STEM faculty to take classes in pedagogy; diversity, equity, and inclusion; and instructional design so that they can successfully implement innovative and socially just STEM education techniques in their own classrooms.

Recent graduate and current Ph.D. student Carter said she would like to see undergraduate STEM education in 2040 allow students to work on topics that resonate with their values, and see education shift from a treatment-focused paradigm to one focused on prevention, which would lead to a solution-focused scientific process. As an example, she asked the symposium participants to imagine working in an environmental justice community in which residents expressed concerns about living close to a Superfund site. Instead of treating every individual that develops cancer from exposure to carcinogens at the site, she proposed cleaning the source of the contamination and getting to the root of the problem.

Another characteristic Carter would like undergraduate STEM education to have by 2040 is for it to be highly interdisciplinary with different tracks, which in her field would include a molecular biology track, an environmental microbiology track, and an environmental policy track. Students could take electives such as scientific journalism, critical race theory, and cultural competency courses, and they would be required to participate in a research project that focuses on a community-specific societal issue. This structure would enable students to learn how to work in a highly collaborative environment, learn critical thinking skills, and learn the value of community expertise, all skills that prospective employers would find valuable.

EXPECTATIONS AND ASSUMPTIONS ABOUT WHO IS INVOLVED IN STEM

After their brief presentations, planning committee member Monique Umphrey of Houston Community College, Northeast led the group in further discussion, beginning by asking Sorensen-Unruh to comment on the assumptions faculty members sometimes bring with them that make it difficult for them to adopt a vision that places students at the center of their educational experiences. Sorensen-Unruh said that a friend of hers talks about how faculty often think of students as cells on a spreadsheet because they are so used to looking at grading sheets that they forget their students are three-dimensional human beings. The challenge, she said, is to look at a student as a complete human being. She has some great Indigenous students at her school, for example, who cannot get a national internship because they have a criminal record, and sponsors of internship programs do not look past that to see someone who has served their time and is very much engaged in their STEM learning process.

Umphrey then asked Weekes to talk about how to expand who is included as a STEM student and STEM professional. The first step, said Weekes, is realizing that not everyone is at the table; she called for everyone to question the current price of admission to the STEM community. As an example, she cited her own experience of having to master either French or German to get her Ph.D. in mathematics. A few universities still have that as a price of admission, even though almost all of the mathematics literature is now in English. Another step is to think seriously about whether all students feel comfortable and welcome in the STEM community.

Responding to a question about how to better engage students today who might not be considering STEM careers, Carter said that the most important thing to do is to make STEM courses relevant to the personal lives of students. For example, she might tell a Black student who comes from a low-wealth community that Black people breathe in 66 percent more air pollution from vehicles than White people (De Moura et al., 2019). She noted that she was able to stay engaged in STEM because she was able to merge her passion for social justice with science, which turned out to be a therapeutic process for her in that it allowed her scientific persona to coexist with her social justice persona. She also pointed to the importance of engaging students in STEM when they are still in elementary school and making internships available for high school students interested in STEM regardless of whether they come from a privileged community or a less well-off one.

When asked to share some of the techniques that her institution, New Mexico Community College, has used to widen the pathway into STEM, Sorensen-Unruh said that digital literacy is an important aspect of building the population of students who enter STEM education. She uses online learning journals as blogs that students can write in regularly to talk about their learning journey or an article that was particularly important or interesting to them that can then start a conversation. She uses ungrading practices (Blum and Kohn, 2020; Schinske and Tanner, 2014) and has students self-evaluate themselves and talk about their growth and the grade they thought they should get based on their effort and time spent on a project or exam. "I try to build metacognition and self-assessment into the classroom so that when students depart from my classroom, they can have not only some knowledge about organic chemistry, but they can also have knowledge about what kind of techniques will be helpful to them in the future," she explained.

Weekes added that she is a proponent of summer research programs such as NSF's Research Experiences for Undergraduates program[4] or the program run by the Mathematical Sciences Research Institute[5] for students who are not highly represented in their disciplines or even their departments. She noted that she has witnessed the students participating in these programs experience surprise and delight at seeing other students that look like them. What is important, though, is to encourage these students to form their own networks and communities so that when they go back to their home institutions, they can continue getting support from their peers.

Planning committee member and Olin College faculty member Stein reflected on the panel discussion and noted that each of the panelists had painted a picture of a future world that is inclusive, meaningful, and connected to one's own experiences. She noted however, that what she sees in

[4]Additional information is available at https://www.nsf.gov/funding/pgm_summ.jsp?pims_id=5517.

[5]Additional information is available at https://www.msri.org/web/msri/education/for-undergraduates/msri-up.

the real world today does not quite look like that. "You may be teaching this way, you may be having these experiences, but that is not ubiquitous across higher education now," said Stein. She asked the panelists to discuss the structures that act as obstacles to making these experiences the rule rather than the exception. Mitra flipped the question around and listed five actions that could make such experiences possible: have a bold vision; create the right team; engage stakeholders across the board, including students, faculty, and representatives from industry; launch programs that aim to change institutional culture; and think and act like a startup. "It is important to recognize that we are talking about culture change and a change of attitude," said Mitra. "We are not talking about changing content and curriculum."

Sorensen-Unruh gave a different answer from her vantage point in the Community College environment: working to get 4-year institutions on board with what she and her colleagues are doing. When she first implemented ungrading, for example, she had to go to the local medical school to get its okay given that most of her students taking organic chemistry were doing so as a prerequisite for applying to medical school. "Until the 4-year community, the graduate school community, and professional school community all buy into some of these techniques that we are talking about, our hands are going to be tied," she explained. She along with Umphrey also noted that many students no longer go to Community College and then a 4-year institution, but rather go back and forth between the two along their educational journey.

Responding to a question about providing support for students in STEM learning pathways, Carter called for an increase in the resources devoted to Minority-Serving Institutions, and to environmental justice work at all types of institutions. She also said that institutions need to increase the number of Black, Indigenous, and other people of color who get tenure. Weekes noted the importance of getting diverse voices at the table to advocate for change and for the adoption of these types of activities. Sorensen-Unruh added that institutions of higher education need to let their faculty be innovative in the ways they instruct their students and stop discouraging experimentation. She also said that educational innovators need to share their ideas and their implementation plans online.

CREATING THE FUTURE

A group of thought leaders and educators was asked to draw on what they had heard during the symposium to imagine a system of undergraduate STEM education as it might look in 2040, a system in which students are well served and well prepared to join the STEM workforce and to navigate the world (see Box 7-2). Panelists were chosen to provide perspectives from

BOX 7-2
Creating the Future We Want

How can we provide flexible and personally relevant undergraduate learning experiences for students?

Panelists:
Susan Singer, Provost, Rollins College
Alegra Eroy-Reveles, Assistant Teaching Professor, Chemistry and Biochemistry, University of California, Santa Cruz
Rufus Glasper, President and CEO, League for Innovation in the Community College
David Soo, Chief of Staff, Jobs for the Future

Moderator:
Kinnis Gosha, Hortenius I. Chenault Endowed Associate Professor, Morehouse College, committee member

academic institutions large and small, as well as nonprofits working to improve education and workforce preparation.

Singer began the session by asking the symposium participants to imagine it was August 2040 and the new academic year was about to launch. Institutions of higher education are still deeply committed to a relevant STEM education that is consciously inclusive, accessible, holistic, flexible, mentored, community-centered, research-centered, filled with rich intellectual experiences, focused on competencies and transferable adaptable skills, supportive of lifelong learning, and filled with curated happenstances that always place the student at the center, but the STEM landscape has changed dramatically in the post-COVID-19 world. In 2040, STEM students enter a higher education system where traditional semesters no longer exist on campuses that no longer have defined borders, information about disciplinary departments can be found in archives, and faculty move in and out of convergent teams focused on grand challenges. Perhaps most importantly, the STEM population in 2040 mirrors the diversity of the nation as a whole.

Continuing to set the scene, Singer said that face-to-face learning is reserved for those situations where person-to-person and person-to-physical environment interactions are absolutely essential and textbook publishers no longer exist. Neuromorphic artificial intelligence has produced efficient digital approaches to analyze cognitive tests, and STEM cognitive tutors abound and are shared widely across the nation. Different cognitive tutors scaffold student learning, measure competencies, and allow aligned progression through collaborative in-person learning opportunities. "That is really the most important and exciting part of the 2040 STEM education," said Singer. With more scaffolded and connected learning, students complete their baccalaureate degree in the equivalent of 3 years, and students move in and out of the educational system through modular approaches that can result in certificates and associate's degrees along the way. In fact, said Singer, the degree itself is on its way to irrelevancy, with digital portfolios serving to demonstrate qualifications and experience.

In this imagined 2040 world, all students—STEM and non-STEM—start their education with a community project that has a STEM dimension such as assessing air quality and the incidence of asthma in mobile homes in which recent immigrants live or working on supply chain management for a local food bank to reduce food spoilage. "Scientists, social scientists, humanists, and artists come together to set the stage for learning in the world of convergence," said Singer. "We have moved past general education to integrated, purposeful learning."

Research projects in 2040, she noted, can be regional and pull multiple institutions together to maximize the use of research instrumentation. Global projects will build on cognitive, tutored language learning and partnerships with global universities abroad or global firms. Partnerships will enhance career opportunities and new financial models, making college accessible financially for everyone.

In response to Singer's presentation about 2040, Eroy-Reveles thanked her for the visionary scenario, and noted that it is flexible, personally relevant, team-based, and engaged with the community. However, Eroy-Reveles noted that the scenario actually presented a deep paradox for her, in that she wants to work on community-engaged projects with a team of faculty, community members, and students, but her reality is teaching 800 general chemistry students for 10 weeks at the University of California, Santa Cruz. "I want to get there," she said, "but there is a deep cultural change that must take place first."

To illustrate that problem, Eroy-Reveles recalled how when she attended her first conference of the Society for Advancement of Chicanos/Hispanics and Native Americans in Science (SACNAS); the organization was celebrating its 30th anniversary. A topic of discussion at that meeting was that since its founding 30 years earlier, the number of Ph.D.s awarded to Hispanics and Native Americans in STEM had only increased from 1 percent to 3 percent. Today, SACNAS is approaching its 50th anniversary, and Eroy-Reveles' guess was that there would only be another small percentage change.

Eroy-Reveles noted that the vision Singer presented challenges colleges and universities to completely reorganize themselves in a way that puts students, their intricacies, and their interconnectedness at the center of the undergraduate experience. Instead of every member being an island unto themselves, this vision will require faculty to move away from individualistic thinking to emphasize collaboration and interdependence. She then wondered which institutions will respond to this challenge and said that it was likely to be those colleges that are already student-centered. "I see the Community Colleges and primarily undergraduate institutions continually asking how can we do better and how can we help our students," said Eloy-Reveles. "They are going to be the ones that drive this change."

One key to achieving equity-focused transformation, she added, will be for STEM education to adopt equity as a primary measure of success, which requires knowing more about who the students are so as to make their education more relevant. She noted that the hiring practices at many institutions, including here, require a diversity statement in employment applications. "This brings in faculty who are very student-centered and who are thinking about our whole population of students," said Eroy-Reveles. Concluding her remarks, she said, "If by 2040, undergraduate institutions, departments, faculty, and granting agencies can adopt equity as our primary measure of success, we will then see our students, and we will serve them with kindness and personally relevant education."

Over the past 3 years in his role with the League for Innovation in the Community College, Glasper said he has been working with the Higher Learning Commission accreditors to create a report that also shared a vision for the future of higher education (Betz et al., 2019). This report concentrated on student-focused engagement and ways in which governance and accreditation can play a role in system transformation. In his view, the most critical goal of undergraduate STEM education is a transition to defining program success by using key performance indicators that measure the cultivation of students who add value to the STEM workforce and their ability to earn a livable wage for a family of four and be successful in their chosen career. He added that by 2040, he would like to see a higher proportion of workers aged 55 and older getting STEM undergraduate degrees, which will place Community Colleges in a lead role in undergraduate STEM education.

Soo, of Jobs for the Future, remarked that one of the things he liked about Singer's vision for 2040 was the idea of cognitive tutors who can take advantage of the many active learning tools that are coming online. In fact, he believes that online education combined with artificial intelligence will make the next generation of learning tools better and more targeted than those available today. He also appreciated the modular approach to STEM education that Singer proposed. His one question was whether a student's learning journey can be done at multiple institutions and venues, including online learning, boot camps and other intensive courses, and apprenticeships and corporate training programs. His general point was that there are so many different types of organizations that will be in the learning business. "I think that once we get better at assessing the quality of learning, I can imagine a more porous learning journey that goes through many different institutions," said Soo. He did note his concern that a radical reimagining of undergraduate STEM education could exacerbate inequities without a laser focus on ensuring better outcomes for underrepresented populations of students.

Planning committee member and Morehouse College faculty member Gosha opened the discussion by asking the panelists to comment on how the STEM learning experience of 2040 could be designed from the start to be more equitable. Soo replied that pathways to a degree need to be more equitable, starting with the search for ways to make sure everyone is prepared to enter those pathways. "As we are developing these alternative pathways and new ways of recognizing learning and going in and out of things, we need to make sure that those are recognized and seen as legitimate," said Soo, "because if they are not seen as legitimate or just as good as, then we are going to be shifting a whole group of people—and we can all guess which people might be shifted into them—into something that is substandard."

Glasper said he would like to see the notion of STEM education expanded to include construction, advanced manufacturing, welding, transportation, and energy, for example. This would give an electrical line worker—the person who climbs poles for the electric company—the opportunity to take classes at a Community College and 4-year institution and get a degree in electrical engineering. Singer noted that NSF's Advance Technology Education program has been trying to do just that for nearly 30 years. What excites her about this avenue into STEM is that it creates the opportunity for industry to share in the expense of a student's education.

Gosha then asked the panelists whether they believe that inequities among student populations will remain in 2040. Glasper said he thinks they will remain at a certain level and that he is not optimistic, seeing how little progress has occurred since he graduated 45 years ago. He sees the lack of what he referred to as a pluralistic system of delivery models as a chief impediment. "We are still looking at delivery models as being the same for every community and the same for every person," said Glasper. "We need to try to look at who the student is and where they come from before focusing the student into the model."

Responding to a question about how the materials that students learn from will change by 2040, Eroy-Reveles suggested that the curriculum will be more integrated and group-based, which she believes will help close equity gaps. Singer said she is hopeful that the uptake of research-based practices will continue, and that today's graduate students will become faculty who use these practices to improve student learning experiences.

Commenting on the connections between academia and industry, Glasper said that he sees this relationship changing and getting stronger with an emphasis on responding to challenges more quickly.

Gosha then asked the panelists whether they thought lifelong learning would be a reality by 2040, and Soo said he could not imagine that it would not be. "If we are going to have a 60-year work life, there are going to be so many things that come out over that time that people will have to learn new skills," said Soo. "The question is whether that education beyond degrees happens at the university or colleges or happens at companies." He said it would behoove colleges and universities to embrace that post-degree market. Doing so, however, will require 4-year institutions to become nimbler and faster at responding to changes in workforce demands. Singer added that she is seeing hints that this is happening already. She noted a nonprofit organization called Credential Engine as a place for those in the workforce to go to get information about lifelong learning opportunities and the value of credentials.[6] She noted that the demographic for those seeking higher education is no longer exclusively those 18 to 22 years old but now includes older working adults.

Posing a question from the symposium participants, Gosha asked the panelists how they would create pathways for humanizing education for faculty today, who the questioner said are ready and willing to move in this direction. Eroy-Reveles replied that creating a community of practice where faculty come together, reflect on what a humanizing education is, and support each other is an important step. Glasper added that breaking education into smaller pieces that allow students to alternate between learning, working to make a living, returning to school for another chunk of education, and so on will help humanize education. He noted that he is working on a project called the Community College Growth Engine Fund[7] that is bringing together six Community Colleges from across the nation to lead a demonstration of how Community Colleges can leverage innovation capacity, regional partnerships, and dynamic labor market data to identify and build subdegree "micropathways" with designated credentials that employers validate. These micropathways will enable learners to earn wages or salaries at or above the median level and stackable credit for degree attainment.

The next question from a symposium participant asked why the decades-old models of interdisciplinary, project-based education developed at Evergreen and Northland have not been adopted elsewhere. This program, explained Singer, uses team-taught courses with faculty from different disciplines and resembles the scenario she painted at the start of the session.

---

[6]Additional information is available at https://credentialengine.org/about/.

[7]Additional information is available at https://eddesignlab.org/project/growthenginefund/.

Barriers to scaling this type of program include financial barriers. Receiving a Pell grant, for example, is conditional on being enrolled in 12 credit hours of courses in a degree program. In addition to state policies that constrain options, she pointed out that it is important that industry recognizes the type of credentials students would get from this type of program.

Soo agreed that there are policy and financial aid issues that need to be resolved because they are not up to the task of supporting innovative approaches to education. He did predict that there would be new financing mechanisms to support nonaccredited programs such as boot camps and credentialing programs. He noted that companies spend many billions of dollars annually on training, and he wondered whether there was a better way of aligning and incentivizing companies to allocate some of those funds to training opportunities in higher education. Singer added that there are isolated examples of institutions developing short-term programs that are funded by mechanisms other than Pell grants and MBA programs funded by businesses rather than by individuals. She also mentioned the need for more public-private partnerships between higher education and industry, and Glasper added that Community Colleges could work with businesses to reach an agreement about credit and noncredit educational opportunities.

Gosha pointed out as a final comment that his institution is the first Historically Black College and University to offer a coding boot camp for its students. His division at Moorhouse College works with industry partners to codevelop courses in computer science.

REDESIGNING THE STUDENT EXPERIENCE

Panelists discussed ways to redesign campuses, classrooms, and learning experiences to align with ambitious goals for the future of STEM education (see Box 7-3). Educators from a variety of institutions including a specialized training school were joined by an architect who works on campus design to share their diverse perspectives on possibilities for future learning.

Gonzaga University dean Annemarie Caño began the panel session by saying that project-based and problem-based learning and crafting experiences designed to solve problems that are meaningful to students bring the interdisciplinary piece into undergraduate STEM education and offer students an opportunity to integrate learning from various disciplines and be more creative. At the same time, she added, it becomes a challenge to prepare students and faculty to engage in a different kind of learning experience. Caño noted that some faculty at her institutions are providing these types of experiences for their students and that NSF is supporting them. Other faculty, however, are happy to be in their disciplinary silos, so it

BOX 7-3
Redesigning the Student Experience

How can we create more accessible and successful student experiences for 2040?

Panelists:
Pam Eddinger, President, Bunker Hill Community College
Amber Luther, Planner and Senior Associate, Populous
Annmarie Caño, Dean, College of Arts and Sciences, Gonzaga University
Michael Roberts, Founder, San Diego Code School

Moderators:
Nicholas Horton, Beitzel Professor in Technology and Society, Amherst College, committee member
Leanne Chukoskie, Director, Power of NeuroGaming (PoNG) Center, University of California, San Diego, committee member

behooves undergraduate institutions to figure out how to respect that desire and still develop lifelong learning experiences for faculty and students and create faculty reward structures that recognize the importance of integrative learning experiences.

Luther, an architect and experienced designer, explained in her remarks that she is one of the leaders of the Campus 2050 Consortium.[8] In her view, the barrier to inclusive, open-source, real-time delivery of education is the current structure of higher education, which she said has not changed much for the past 900 to 1,000 years. What she would like to see is a new structure that marries workforce development with people and institutions of higher education so that artificial intelligence, technology, and individual relationships help shape a student wanting to go to university for something specific, employers wanting to target a specific talent, and universities that provide the right outcomes and opportunities for the students. This approach would make partnerships more holistic, help curate student learning over their lifetime, and help students stay engaged in lifetime learning as their careers evolve.

From his perspective as founder of San Diego Code School, Roberts said that the COVID-19 pandemic has accelerated the process of reimagining what undergraduate STEM education will look like in the future. In his opinion, undergraduate institutions need to figure out each student's "superpower" that can help them make a big impact in the workforce and

[8]Additional information is available at https://populous.com/making-case-innovation-districts.

also reimagine how they can create environments that are more supportive of and centered around students. This, he said, comes down to identifying the types of wraparound services each individual needs to be successful. It also requires higher education to pivot and constantly recalibrate what students need to get a good job that adds meaning to their lives. He then questioned why institutions of higher education do not cooperate more with STEM employers to determine the skills that students need to master.

Eddinger noted that Community Colleges, such as Bunker Hill Community College where she is the president, are educating close to half of all U.S. undergraduates, and these students will constitute the foundation of the 2040 workforce. Some 65 to 70 percent of the students at these institutions are from underrepresented groups and are primarily first-generation students from low-income populations. The changing makeup of this population, she said, will affect Community Colleges in 2040 in that more adult students will attend community colleges and the majority of these "nontraditional" Community College students will be working as they go to school.

She explained that students in 2040 will be going in and out of the workforce, and what will not change is the attractiveness of STEM for these students. "My students know that STEM is going to be providing their new jobs," said Eddinger, and yet people of color, women, and adults are not seen as prime candidates for the jobs of the future. She then described a program organized by the New England Venture Capital Association called Hack Diversity, which takes cohorts of Community College students of color and women and matches them with employers in the computer science and information technology fields. At first, she said, employers were reluctant to take on students who did not already know what they were doing, but after three or four cohorts went through the programs, it was clear that companies were hiring these students after they completed this internship program. The important point, she said in her concluding comments, is to understand where students are coming from and what their goals in life are.

BUILDING TOWARD THE VISION

Planning committee member and Amherst College faculty member Horton opened the discussion by asking the panelists how they would introduce the many necessary, people-intensive changes that have been discussed in a sustainable manner given the financial constraints facing institutions of higher education at all levels. Eddinger said the easy answer is to get foundation funding, ask industry for money, and in short, be innovative in how education is funded. Ultimately, though, if undergraduate STEM education is ever to be foundational for a vibrant U.S. economy, federal and state governments will have to stop disinvesting in public higher education. One key to making that happen, she said, is to drive home the message that public higher education is a public good, an idea with which Luther agreed.

For Roberts, the solution to having undergraduate STEM education serve the public good is to not only to support all of the suggested changes the discussions have highlighted but also to pay students, particularly those that wanting retraining or upskilling, and those students who come from disadvantaged backgrounds. The source of those funds could be industry if companies can be persuaded to reinvest some of the money they spend now on recruiting and in-house retraining into cooperative education models.

Caño pointed to the importance of supporting faculty through all of the changes that the future of STEM education will require to create a more inclusive, diverse, and meaningful educational system. "If we want them to transform the way they are teaching, we need to make sure they have the time and energy to do so," she said. She also noted that interdisciplinary teaching and team teaching are important ways to support faculty and that they want to engage each other in this way. Caño urged an allotment of time and space to give faculty the latitude to test approaches to this type of teaching, which can also serve as a means of breaking down silos and sharing knowledge across disciplines. She suggested incorporating STEM-based, service-learning experiences into the undergraduate experience.

Horton agreed that team teaching should be an important part of the undergraduate STEM educational system. He added that the pathways into and out of Community Colleges, 4-year institutions, and the workplace need to be smoother and become a standard part of the educational system. Luther said she believes universities, where the free flow of information and collaboration should be happening, should be places where interdisciplinary teaching and team teaching should occur naturally. The challenge will be breaking down the silos that exist between the university ecosystem and the workplace ecosystem.

Roberts sees the changing of the guard between now and 2040 as being an incredibly important prerequisite for future change. He noted that the current generation of students is serious about social change, and he predicted that these younger faculty and administrators will drive change from the bottom up and support the innovation needed to create the educational ecosystem that students and the U.S. economy need.

Eddinger said that she hopes that the next 20 years will involve the best dismantling of higher education ever, particularly the dismantling of privilege regarding both race and ethnicity and the privilege elite institutions take for granted. "I would like to see the dismantling of faculty space and administration space in such a way that we see the components that are good and that the work that we do then is in the reassembling of it," she said. She also called for creating more local hubs that can work together to serve their communities, work together to improve the educational system, and work together to scale programs that work locally.

8

Final Reflections

The symposium was structured to allow participants to pause at various points to reflect on how panel discussions built on each other and take stock of how they might fit together into an agenda for action. Participants were invited, for example, to participate in small breakout session discussions and to imagine and write stories about the future. The symposium began to wrap up with a panel of several participants who were invited to offer their own ideas for sharing the ideas discussed at the symposium more widely to the broader higher education community and beyond. Final thoughts were offered by Robin Wright as a representative of the National Science Foundation, the project sponsor, and from the committee co-chairs, Annette Parker and Barbara Schaal.

EXAMPLES OF PARTICIPANT STORIES

Symposium participants were offered the opportunity to engage in multiple exercises to discuss and then write stories imagining the future of undergraduate STEM students in 2040. Suggested story topics for group writing included reenvisioning courses; internships, cooperatives, and work experience; capstone and integrative experiences; informal and continuing education; and cocurricular and service-learning projects. Committee member Leanne Chukoskie shared some of the insights from the stories generated at the symposium. The STEM students of 2040, she began, will not necessarily come straight from high school, and the prominence of lifelong learning and solving problems relevant to the communities in which students live permeated many of the stories. These students of the future, she added, will be seeking missions, not majors, and will be looking for blending opportunities that meld traditional higher education learning opportunities with paid opportunities in industry. Coursework will be more competency-based and will be built with the mindset that many learners will not have the time to be full-time, traditional students. Competencies in these stories reflected both national standards and local, community needs, and all learners will have access to a success coach so that they can make sure that their learning remains a priority regardless of other things that are going on in their life. Higher education will focus on the goal of moving people quickly from learning into the workforce.

Committee member Nicholas Horton said that he heard shared ideas about how students in 2040 will experience creative assessments that measure critical thinking and learning in context rather than the ability to memorize facts. Courses, then, will be collaborative and feature problem-based learning and experiential activities that cross disciplines and will require teamwork. Internships, cooperatives, capstone projects, and practica will provide students with multiple integrative experiences as means for developing the capacities needed in the workplace. Achieving this vision requires faculty who are willing enough to engage with other disciplines within their institutions and within industry. The story writers, said Horton, also envisioned a type of continuing education that would be more flexible, independent, and engaged with the community.

PARTICIPANT PERSPECTIVES: BUILDING ON CURRENT INNOVATIONS

Several symposium participants contributed their individual perspectives on how undergraduate STEM might look in 2040. Topics included imagining the world of 2040, transforming the student learning experience, redesigning pathways for undergraduate STEM education, systemic change in higher education, and envisioning the future role of faculty and staff. Two examples of stories can be found in Boxes 8-1 and 8-2, others can be found on the symposium webpage.[1]

The moderators created a word cloud summarizing key ideas and themes from the individual stories (Figure 8-1) and also offered reflections on the story writing exercise. Commenting on the stories she read, planning committee member Lynn Andrea Stein said she was happy that education, learning, and students appear in the middle of the word cloud, and pleased that the words surrounding them—whole-person, interdisciplinary, flexible, inclusive, collaborative, partnering, work, justice, and individualized—are

[1] https://www.nationalacademies.org/event/10-21-2020/imagining-the-future-of-undergraduate-stem-education-symposium.

BOX 8-1
Student Mission in 2040

Imagine coming to school and declaring your mission instead of a major. Students will join supportive communities in which mentors help them choose a path of courses, experiences, and projects that will help them to build the skills, abilities, and mindsets they need to achieve their mission, including interdisciplinary competence, the ability to think in context in a way that takes awareness of larger systems into account, an understanding of people and cultures on a global scale, experience solving problems and implementing solutions in the community, and the use of inquiry to follow personal curiosities. Faculty will run projects and create modules to help students learn fundamentals and integrate their learning. Various pathways through education will be grouped by theme—sustainability, joyful living, health, infrastructure, for instance—rather than discipline. When students leave school, they will have a collection of credentials, portfolios, and artifacts of their work in addition to a possible degree.

SOURCE: Submission at the symposium by C.J. McClelland, teaching associate professor and director of Grand Challenges scholars, Colorado School of Mines.

BOX 8-2
Student Experience via Online Learning

Next week I'll be getting my college degree! I'm an immigrant and my parents never attended college, but I've known since middle school that I could attend college because it is a matter of being interested, and there is no cost to me or my family. I did some of my college classes online while I was in high school, and then I attended my local Community College for a year because my mom was sick and I needed to be home to take care of her. I also took some more courses online, though. During that first summer I participated in a research experience program that allowed me to work in my community and gain college credit.

The learning experiences that I've engaged in are all part of my online portfolio. When I decided to begin attending a university, I picked up my learning right where my portfolio left off at that point. I've had project-based courses, small group courses, and service-learning projects in the community. Every summer, I had the opportunity to do an internship in a different industry to find out what type of work I'd like to do. Through it all, I've been able to stay connected with a cohort of my fellow students with shared interests and experiences. I can't wait to get into the workforce and start contributing! And the best part is that I know I'll be able to keep building my portfolio as I gain new and different skills through the years.

SOURCE: Submission at the symposium by Gabriela C. Weaver, professor of chemistry, University of Massachusetts, Amherst.

FIGURE 8-1 Word cloud summarizing the key ideas and themes from group discussions regarding the future of undergraduate STEM education.

themes expressed repeatedly throughout the symposium. She also noted that joy, immersion, and curiosity were new ideas coming out of the discussions. "As STEM professionals, I think we all like to believe those are at the center of the education that we envision for our students," said Stein.

Stein said there is an opportunity to create an undergraduate STEM educational experience that recognizes individual students where they are, takes a system approach, and changes the world by changing the educational system. At the same time, another theme Stein heard throughout the conversations of the past 2 days was that when making a change to one piece of the system, other parts of the system tend to pull it back to the status quo. "In some ways, some of the changes we have been talking about in the last 2 days we have been talking about for a pretty long time, and this may be a moment where there is enough disruption in the system that we can finally begin to rethink the system itself and not the practices of particular components within the system," she said.

Stein reiterated the message of being cautious not to introduce changes that can introduce new inequities, yet she also noted the optimism that this is a moment to begin building a different kind of STEM education, one that is not about ivory-tower science, isolated ideas, or intellect, but instead about the ways in which ideas of STEM, as well as the arts, humanities, social sciences, business, and entrepreneurial thinking, come together to solve society's big problems.

Ortiz then reflected on the discussions by noting that society today is increasingly rife with social inequities, planetary perils, and the realization that the collective impact of humans threatens life on earth and is transforming societies and ecosystems. "We have seen that while science and technology has contributed enormous benefits to humanity, it is simultaneously entangled with and has contributed to all of these challenges that we face," said Ortiz.

Having embarked on the effort needed to reimagine a more equitable and sustainable future, a theme that comes through, she said, is the need to acknowledge, interrogate, and strive to understand the historical context, root causes, and systemic structures that underpin the scientific and technological enterprise, as well as the institutions of higher learning that serve as its foundation. "Inequity in higher education, including access and quality and the nature of education, is a growing challenge, and as we take on the bold endeavor of tackling these enduring problems of humanity, we also must be reflective of humanity," Ortiz remarked, adding that while the discussions on equity have emphasized a lack of representation, this is a surface symptom of much deeper root causes, she added.

Planning committee member Christine Ortiz of MIT and Station1 then offered a few ideas that could elevate the best parts of human nature within STEM to lift humanity into a new collective and moral consciousness. The first step, she said, is to interrogate what foundational knowledge and the canon of individual discipline actually means and to integrate respect for different ways of knowing into the core foundations and canon of disciplines. "We need to reflect upon the flaws and intentional approaches to reform underlying mindsets and values in our institutions," said Ortiz. "This includes concepts of meritocracy, rigor, excellence, deficit, frames, flaws in the pipeline metaphor, technological determination, and even innovation and disruption."

She concluded her remarks by noting the importance of understanding the perils, scenarios, and potential futures that are more inequitable, elevate racism, and are mechanical and dehumanizing. "We have to realize that our choices of pathways are not mutually exclusive, that there is promise and peril in every pathway." Her suggestion was to have another symposium that would look at a dystopian version of the past 2 days.

Next, planning committee co-chair Annette Parker of South Central College shared her view of the symposium's discussions from her perspective as a Community College president. She reflected on the first commissioned paper presented by Lindsey Malcom-Piqueux (see Chapter 3) and considered Malcom-Piqueux's research on equity and the importance of creating a future that supports diversity and equity reflecting the diverse nation the United States has become as very powerful. Parker pointed out that today's undergraduate STEM education system does not reflect the diversity of the population and she also noted the need to create a flexible ecosystem for learning that takes into account career transitions and lifelong learning and provides on- and off-ramps that empower rather than impede students in using their diversity and human potential to deal with real-world problems in their communities. Undergraduate STEM education, she added, must be multidisciplinary, include critical thinking and active learning, and deal with societal issues, and accreditation programs need to support this new vision for undergraduate STEM education.

To conclude the day, planning committee co-chair Barbara Schaal of Washington University in St. Louis offered some of the ideas from the two days of discussion that she found interesting. The first was about integrating neuroscience into education to better understand the biological basis of implicit bias and a host of other behaviors and to leverage neuroplasticity to effect changes in behavior. She noted how the institutions that serve those from groups that are underrepresented in STEM today—Historically Black College and Universities (HBCUs) and tribal colleges, specifically—are very good at taking students from incredibly diverse backgrounds, working with and supporting them, and seeing them through to matriculation. She reiterated the idea that these institutions have lessons from which the rest of the undergraduate STEM education system could benefit. Schaal stressed that admitting someone to college or university is not the same as educating them.

The idea of an ecosystem of learning was particularly interesting to Schaal, as was the need to operate this ecosystem using democratized data and information. This ecosystem should be personalized in the way that Instagram and TikTok are, and in fact, she suggested that those social media platforms could hold lessons for the undergraduate STEM education community. The ecosystem of learning will depend heavily on the Internet, raising the importance of providing broadband access and the tools to use it to all Americans—rural and urban—if equity is the goal, as well as on the availability of effective educational modules of the type seen in well-resourced schools. She also commented on the need to make undergraduate STEM education relevant to students and involve them in solving problems that are important in their communities

POSSIBLITIES FOR THE FUTURE

As a concluding activity, the planning committee asked educators who had participated in the symposium to summarize the lessons they drew from the discussions and activities and to offer suggestions for sharing these insights more widely (see Box 8-3).

BOX 8-3
Possibilities for the Future

What actions would help with efforts to improve undergraduate STEM learning?

Panelists:
Brendan Kern, Associate Professor of Biology and Teacher Advisor, Johnson C. Smith University
Kai Jun Chew, Ph.D. Candidate, Virginia Tech
Cordelia Ontiveros, Professor Emerita, California State Polytechnic University, Pomona
Patrick Shabram, Professor, Front Range Community College
Bob Kolvoord, Dean, College of Integrated Science and Engineering, James Madison University
Jessica Parr, Associate Professor (teaching) of chemistry, University of Southern California
Erika Steele, Research Associate, University of Alabama
Mica Estrada, Associate Professor, University of California, San Francisco

Moderator:
Ryan Kelsey, Executive Director, Partnership Development, the Markle Foundation

Kern said that one big change he would like to see is to have the ability to customize education to meet the student where they are and to have a pathway that works for them and their goals. He noted that institutions of higher education will have to get innovative with how they use technology to enable adaptable timelines and more flexible curricula, while the United States is going to have to find new and sustainable ways to fund schools and pay for education that do not rely on the semester system or financially penalize students who do not follow the traditional timeline. "There are strong social justice implications because it gives an opening to repair the damage done by a racially and financially biased school and employment system to help students meet their potential and use their skills to best effect," said Kern. He also noted that students today want to make a difference. "Yes, they need a job that pays the bills, but it is not enough. They want to rebuild the world, so we should give them the tools," he said.

When COVID-19 restrictions are relaxed, he would like to see several changes in undergraduate STEM education, starting with programs that adopt more flexible curricula. This is something schools could do immediately, and though it would require more personalized mentoring, this is something that most Minority-Serving Institutions (MSIs) and Community Colleges already have in place and from which other institutions could learn, said Kern. Also needed, he said, is better-coordinated transfers between schools so that students do not lose credits, time, and money. He also called for the undergraduate STEM education community to stop focusing on "major" institutions because they are not doing a good job with students from minoritized populations. "They will often use money to attract students who would otherwise maybe go to some of these smaller institutions, but they do not have the outcomes to show that they are actually supporting those students the way that some of our smaller institutions could do," said Kern.

The conversation with employers will need to change as well, he said. "We cannot become job-training services, given how variable the workplace and the future in general will be. We need to be focused on widely applicable transferable skills, and if industry wants this training, then maybe that happens on their end," Kern stated. "Much of the inequality that we see our students struggling with was caused by the very industry structures that we were sometimes asked to support, and we need to ask ourselves if it is ethical to consider supporting those structures."

Ph.D. candidate Chew of the University of Virginia said he hopes that over the next 20 years, there is a paradigm shift in assessing learning. Such a shift is needed to enable more team-based active learning experiences, allow students to customize their learning pathways, and address social justice concerns. He noted that there has been a substantial body of research on assessment from which the undergraduate STEM education community can draw. When COVID-19 restrictions end, Chew would like to see more research on how to assess faculty teaching skills and the reasons why instructors prefer particular types of assessment.

A key lesson that excited Cordelia Ontiveros, the emerita dean of the Engineering at Cal Poly Pomona, is that undergraduate STEM education is becoming more socially and culturally aware, equitable, and inclusive. She is also excited about a future where multiple, valid pathways are available for students to pursue an undergraduate STEM education; their background and experience are considered to be valid, relevant, and important, students are accepted where they are; and diverse students can experience a sense of belonging, community, and acknowledgment that they matter and count as competent STEM students.

Ontiveros said that when the COVID-19 restrictions end, she plans to use the structures and contents of this symposium in her classes. She said the symposium has highlighted multiple ways of interacting with presenters and attendees, and she thinks these different avenues—articles available to read in advance, presentations and discussion, small group breakouts around specific questions, shared documents for recording thoughts, discussion boards for sharing and responding to ideas—will allow for a better learning experience for students, one that involves them more in their own education.

Patrick Shabram of Front Range Community College said he is most excited about the increasing number of inclusive internships and research experiences that target or at least encourage participation by students from underrepresented groups as well as first- and second-year students, including Community College students. “Not only do these programs give students real-world experience, they often solidify the students’ decisions to pursue a STEM major in the first place, which is why it is so important that we reach these students early,” said Shabram. An important development he sees is that many of these opportunities are paid experiences, which is important because it does not place socioeconomic limitations on students. He hopes to see more government agencies, more nonprofits, and more private companies hiring Community College and first- and second-year students into paid internships. Shabram noted that he was going to take the COVID-19 restrictions as an opportunity to rethink everything about the way he organizes his classes.

Turning to the second group of four panelists, planning committee member Ryan Kelsey of the Markle Foundation asked the panelists to discuss what excites them most about how undergraduate STEM education will change by 2040 and what they see as good ways of disseminating the lessons from this symposium. James Madison University’s Kolvoord said he was excited about the continuing movement to place the student and problem-solving at the center of undergraduate STEM education, rather than faculty and the discipline. This change is already allowing the system to focus on all learners, particularly those who have not been the center of attention to date. He wonders, though, what the catalyst will be to make this change spread throughout higher education, particularly after the pandemic is over.

Regarding dissemination, he would like to see the focus be on Community Colleges and HBCUs rather than on the few institutions that today get most of the attention. There also needs to be outreach to legislators and other federal and state government officials because they make budget decisions that affect what can be done on campus. “Most of us, sadly, are not beneficiaries of billion-dollar endowments, and it is going to take resources to make some of these changes,” said Kolvoord. Without the support of stakeholders, he worries that the system will act like a rubber band that will stretch but then snap back to where it was.

University of Southern California’s Parr said she is excited about shifting the role of instructors from being content deliverers to becoming guides who show how to use content effectively. “Our students have all of the knowledge for general chemistry in their pocket on their cell phone,” said Parr. “My job now has shifted from giving them that content into how they use it and apply it to real-world problems.” She agreed with Kolvoord that outreach to stakeholders is important, as is the creation of spaces to bring people together for sharing information. For her, bringing together all the stakeholders who affect undergraduate education, including those researchers who study best practices in education, is an important step toward changing the culture of undergraduate STEM education. These communities of learning could be an effective dissemination mechanism.

University of Alabama's Steele, who evaluates programs for undergraduate learning, said she would like to see education that is equitable and gives every student the same opportunity to success when they get to college. Achieving that goal means meeting students where they are, perhaps by partnering with K–12 schools to help provide opportunities for all schools. As an example, she compared the K–12 school where her son goes versus the one her nephew attends. One of the schools sends the kids to science camp, while the other school cannot afford textbooks for every child. She also called on research-oriented universities to do a better job helping students embrace their identities in higher education.

In terms of dissemination, Steele, who is a science education researcher, agreed with Parr that networking and learning communities that go beyond academic silos and discipline-specific meetings will be critical for getting best practices into the hands of more instructors. Workshops and professional development opportunities for faculty are also needed. She would also like to see more partnerships with the business community and the larger community in which students live to better understand what they expect from students.

Mica Estrada of the University of California, San Francisco noted that historically, higher education has used tests and grades to identify talent who can contribute to expanding and strengthening the national economy. She would like to see a shift from identifying talent to developing talent equitably, and this talent development would include imparting not only foundational knowledge but also metacognitive abilities and human virtues. A second shift would be to turn from focusing on national economic growth to the well-being of people and the planet. In her view, that shift would move the system away from exploiting people, which she said happens in academia. Such a shift would help students grow and contribute equitably to the common good and would begin to decolonize academia and make space for other ways of knowing, something that is essential for achieving equity in academia.

As a communications strategist, Estrada said the first step in any dissemination effort has to be to understand the different audiences, including those at institutions of higher education who control faculty reward structures. Other important audiences include business, community organizations, and politicians, as well as accreditation agencies, the annual *U.S. News & World Report* ranking of colleges and universities, and funders. The second step is then to think about content and stories about people to illustrate that content. "If you want to shift norms, I would lead with concrete stories and concrete data that demonstrate the most efficacious things we have been talking about," said Estrada. At the same time, she said, it is important to focus on what is known as WIIFM (what's in it for me)? The other two important considerations are the mode for delivering the message and the duration of the messaging activities.

Her final point was to convey to stakeholders that the necessary paradigm shift is not concerned with money but instead with the well-being and health of the academic community, the local community, and the environment. If administrators are the audience, for example, inform them that these changes are needed to benefit the well-being and health of everyone on campus. "I would start that discussion and let them generate ideas on how they would make that shift happen," Estrada said in closing the session.

CLOSING REMARKS

The symposium closed with reflections from the sponsor, Robin Wright, director of the Division on Undergraduate Education at the National Science Foundation (NSF), and the committee co-chairs, Annette Parker and Barbara Schaal.

Wright noted that many of those attending the symposium have worked hard at improving undergraduate STEM education for decades and that much has changed over the past 20 years. The incremental changes that have occurred, though, are not going to be enough to propel the vision of undergraduate STEM education that emerged from this symposium.

Wright pointed out some basic truths that emerged from the symposium. First, there is a need to measure what really matters in ways that are fair, equitable, and authentic to STEM from grading lab work to measuring the quality of the curriculum. Measuring what matters means stating what success in a STEM course, curriculum, or discipline means. One critical measure is a determination about who is included and excluded from STEM. "To achieve the inclusion, equity, and diversity that we have been talking about, yearning for, and desperately need, we have to measure the impacts of STEM education beyond averages to their impacts on groups of students and on individuals," said Wright.

The second basic truth is that undergraduate STEM education must empower students, and empowerment needs to be a defining feature of the undergraduate STEM education system of the future. It was noted multiple times during the symposium that students need to work on relevant projects right from the start and not wait until they earn credentials before starting to change the world. The STEM education of 2040 needs to be a place where students can begin to become the change makers, the world improvers, and the solution developers that the world needs, said Wright.

NSF, said Wright, is ready to support efforts to turn the vision for undergraduate STEM education painted at this symposium into a reality. She challenged the symposium participants to think big, to envision large-scale efforts that could propel undergraduate STEM education forward toward goals that enable all learners to be STEM-knowledgeable and able to seek STEM careers. "What large-scale efforts would bring the country from the level it is now to provide the diversity of thought and talent to achieve the future we would like to see in 2040?" she asked, adding that the nation cannot wait for solutions. "The needs are too urgent and the consequences of business as usual are too dire," she said in concluding her remarks.

Parker agreed with Wright that big changes are needed and said that the paper from Malcom-Piqueux affected her more than anything she heard in that it talked about how the legislation that was intended to help all of the nation's citizens instead had produced unintended consequences that did not make education equitable so that all students could succeed. In terms of making big changes, the ability of colleges and universities across the country to switch rapidly from in-person education to remote education shows that the nation's institutions of higher education can make big changes when they put their minds to it. She then noted, too, that the social unrest that occurred during the summer of 2020 has brought to the fore issues of equity, inclusion, and justice, and illustrated clearly that students will not tolerate inequitable situations anymore.

Coming from her perspective as a college president, Parker said that the accreditation process is often looked at as something that limits change, but her institution's recent experience with accreditation suggests that there are opportunities to make big changes if the accreditation agencies are clued into what is coming in the future. She suggested, in fact, that accreditation agencies be on the list of organizations that the symposium's dissemination efforts include.

Returning to Malcom-Piqueux's paper, Parker said that it helped her understand that throughout the nation's history, not all Black students such as herself made it through the system, and it was due to unintentional roadblocks. "What we do in the future," said Parker, "we cannot make that mistake again. We need to understand where those limits are and how everybody gets on the train."

In her summary, Schaal highlighted another story from a symposium participant who pointed out that everything that happens in higher education is contained within a system that has a structure with advantages and disadvantages that are clearly defined along racial lines. It is therefore essential to disrupt and dismantle that system to benefit future students while at the same time continuing to educate today's students. "We are not just building a plane, we are building it while we are flying it," said

Schaal. On a final note, she added that there are bright lights in the system, particularly regarding how many HBCUs and tribal universities are doing a good job working with students and moving them along an educational journey in a very individual way using dynamic structures that focus on equitable learning and outcomes.

References

Betz, D., C. Bustamante, S. Davidson, R. Glasper, T. Hartle, S. Jenkins, C. Johnson-Odim, A. Levine, R. McMahan, M. Milliron, L. Milne, M. Murdock, E. Sibolski, L. Skogen, T. Slottow, B. Smith, R. Stein, W. Tammone, J. Webb, D. Wendler, and D. Wissman. 2019. *Innovation: Beyond the horizon and the future of higher education.* Chicago, IL: Higher Learning Commission.

Blum, S.D., and A. Kohn. 2020. *Ungrading: Why rating students undermines learning (and what to do instead).* Morgantown: West Virginia University Press.

Bureau of Labor Statistics. 2020. *Employment projections: Employment in STEM occupations.* https://www.bls.gov/emp/tables/stem-employment.htm.

Cech, E.A., and M. Blair-Loy. 2019. The changing career trajectories of new parents in STEM. *Proceedings of the National Academy of Sciences* 116(10):4182-4187. doi: 10.1073/pnas.1810862116.

Cech, E.A., B. Rubineau, S. Silbey, and C. Seron. 2011. Professional role confidence and gendered persistence in engineering. *American Sociological Review* 76(5):641-666.

Cech, E.A., A. Metz, J.L. Smith, and K. deVries. 2017. Epistemological dominance and social inequality: Experiences of Native American science, engineering, and health students. *Science, Technology, & Human Values* 42(5):743-774.

Cech, E.A., M. Blair-Loy, and L.E. Rogers. 2018a. Recognizing chilliness: How schemas of inequality shape views of culture and climate in work environments. *American Journal of Cultural Sociology* 6(1):125-160.

Cech, E.A., J.L. Smith, and A. Metz. 2018b. Cultural processes of ethnoracial disadvantage among Native American college students. *Social Forces* 98(1):355-380.

de Moura, P., M. Cecilia, and D. Reichmuth. 2019. *Inequitable exposure to air pollution from vehicles in the northeast and mid-Atlantic.* Cambridge, MA: Union of Concerned Scientists.

Fletcher, E., and W. Tyson. 2017a. Bridging technical skills gaps between high school students and local employers. *Journal of Research in Technical Careers* 1(1):20-31.

Fletcher, E., and W. Tyson. 2017b. A longitudinal analysis of young adult pathways to STEMH occupations. *Career and Technical Education Research* 42(1):35-55.

National Academies of Sciences, Engineering, and Medicine (NASEM). 2018a. *Engineering societies' activities in promoting diversity and inclusion: Proceedings of a workshop–in brief*. Edited by S. Olson and K. Jarboe. Washington, DC: The National Academies Press.

———. 2018b. *Sexual harassment of women: Climate, culture, and consequences in academic sciences, engineering, and medicine*. Edited by P.A. Johnson, S.E. Widnall, and F.F. Benya. Washington, DC: The National Academies Press.

———. 2020. *Promising practices for addressing the underrepresentation of women in science, engineering, and medicine: Opening doors*. Edited by R. Colwell, A. Bear, and A. Helman. Washington, DC: The National Academies Press.

National Science Board. 2020. *Vision 2030*. Alexandria, VA: National Science Board.

Núñez, A.-M., J. Rivera, and T. Hallmark. 2020. Applying an intersectionality lens to expand equity in the geosciences. *Journal of Geoscience Education* 68(2):97-114.

Núñez, A.-M., J. Posselt, T. Hallmark, J. Rivera, and D. Southern. 2021. The organization of learning in geoscience fieldwork and implications for inclusion. *Journal of Women and Minorities in Science and Engineering*.

Sansone, V., A.-M. Núñez, J.K. Haschenburger, A. Godet, W. Gray, M.B. Suarez, S. Birnbaum, and D. Young. 2019. Developing work-based geosciences learning opportunities in a Hispanic-serving institution. *New Directions for Student Services* 2019(167):85-99.

Schinske, J., and K. Tanner. 2014. Teaching more by grading less (or differently). *CBE Life Sciences Education* 13(2):159-166.

Selingo, J.J. 2018. *The new generation of students: How colleges can recruit, teach, and serve Gen Z*. Washington, DC: Chronicle of Higher Education.

Smith, C.A.S. 2017. Community colleges as a pathway for low income women to enter the engineering technology workforce. In *Gender (in)equality: Stalled revolutions and shifting terrains in the 21st century* (pp. 28-47) edited by S.N. Davis, S. Winslow, and D.J. Maume. Oakland, CA: University of California Press.

Smithsonian Institution. 2021. *The STEM imperative*. https://ssec.si.edu/stem-imperative.

Tyson, W., E. Fletcher, D. Orozco, and L. Jayaram. 2018. *PathTech Life all respondents: 2018 report*. Tampa: University of South Florida.

Villa, E.Q., S. Hug, H. Thiry, D.S. Knight, E.F. Hall, and A. Tirres. 2019. *Broadening participation of Hispanics in computing: The CAHSI Includes Alliance*. Paper presented at Annual Collaborative Network for Engineering and Computing (CoNECD) at the American Society for Engineering Education, Washington, DC.

World Economic Forum (WEF). 2020. *The future of jobs report*. Cologny, Switzerland: World Economic Forum.

Appendix A

Statement of Task

A workshop planning committee will plan and hold a public symposium on the future of undergraduate science, technology, engineering, and mathematics (STEM) education and will draw on research and highlight successful programs to engage educators, researchers, higher education administrators, policy makers, funders, and representatives from industry in conversations about how to improve undergraduate STEM learning. The focus will be on undergraduate STEM education in 2040 and beyond in the context of the convergence of STEM disciplines and the changes in the population, goals, and pathways of undergraduate STEM students. The symposium may address the following questions and may be refined by the planning process.

- How can undergraduate STEM education respond to the rapidly changing context for higher education—calls for convergence, demographic and societal changes, changes in workforce demands, advances in technology—in ways that anticipate future demands and provide quality education for all students?
- What changes are needed to undergraduate STEM education in light of the increasing convergence across STEM? What are critical convergent topics and approaches that we urgently need to incorporate into undergraduate STEM education?
- What are the models, both administrative and financial, that support a convergent learning experience that engages multiple disciplines and overarching concerns such as privacy, security, and ethical behavior of people and systems?

- Is there a relationship between content, delivery mechanism, use of technology in the classroom/learning environment and success of first-generation and low-income STEM students of any background? Is the relationship different for different groups? What would it mean to design changes based on an equity and social justice mindset from start?
- How should the STEM education system respond to the changes taking place in the learning pathways of individuals at different points of their lives, including enrolling at different physical and online institutions, and/or stacking credentials and experiences from multiple sources? How can we consider learning in contexts other than formal settings, for different cultures, ages, or levels of instruction?

The workshop committee will define the specific topics to be addressed, develop the agenda, and select and invite speakers and other participants. After the workshop, a proceedings of the workshop presentations and discussions will be prepared by a designated rapporteur in accordance with institutional guidelines.

Appendix B

Symposium Agenda

Symposium on Imagining the Future of Undergraduate STEM Education

National Academies of Sciences, Engineering, and Medicine
Board on Science Education
Board on Higher Education and Workforce

Pre-Symposium Activities:

Posting and Discussion of Idea Competition Winners
Posting and Discussion of Commissioned Papers

Thursday, November 12

11:00 ET **Welcome and Vision of the Future**

The importance of undergraduate STEM education and how changes in science, technology, economics, and society coming in the next 20 to 40 years should drive changes in undergraduate STEM learning.

- Marcia McNutt, President, National Academy of Sciences
- F. Fleming Crim, Chief Operating Officer, National Science Foundation
- Annette Parker, President, South Central College, committee co-chair
- Barbara Schaal, Mary Dell Chilton Distinguished Professor, Washington University in St. Louis, committee co-chair

11:30 **Changing Landscapes: 2040 vs 2020**

Rethinking how we see the history of higher education and pivoting to how and why undergraduate STEM education will (and should) look very different in 20 years than it does today.

Presentation on Commissioned Paper: **Transformational Moments in U.S. Higher Education: Implications for Racial Equity**

Lindsey Malcom-Piqueux, Senior Institutional Research Analyst, Caltech

Panelists:
- Vicki Chandler, Provost and Chief Academic Officer, Minerva
- Mark Mitsui, President, Portland Community College
- Tonya Matthews, Director of STEM Learning Innovation and Assoc. Provost for Inclusive Workforce Development, Wayne State University
- Vicente Talanquer, Distinguished Professor, University of Arizona
- Lindsey Malcom-Piqueux, Senior Institutional Research Analyst, Caltech

Moderator:
Annette Parker, President, South Central College, committee co-chair

12:30 **STEM Education for What? Goals for the Future**

What purposes does undergraduate STEM education serve now and how will (should) that change in the future?

Panelists:
- William F. Tate IV, Provost, University of South Carolina
- Eloy Oakley, Chancellor, California Community College System
- Wanda Sigur, Lockheed Martin (retired)
- Francis Su, Benediktsson-Karwa Professor of Mathematics, Harvey Mudd College

Moderators:
- Arthur Lee, Fellow and Principal Advisor, Chevron Services Company, committee member
- Cathy Manduca, Director, Science Education Resource Center, Carleton College, committee member

1:30 Break

2:00 **STEM Education for Whom?**
A look at current research and trend data on equity, inclusion, and outcomes for undergraduate STEM students at various types of institutions.

Presenters:
- Anne Marie Núñez, Professor of Educational Studies, The Ohio State University
- Will Tyson, Associate Professor of Sociology, University of South Florida
- Erin Cech, Assistant Professor of Sociology, University of Michigan

Moderator:
Josipa Roksa, Director of Strategic Academic Programs and Professor of Sociology and Education, University of Virginia

2:45 **Creating Inclusive Higher Education for STEM Students of the Future**
Opportunity for participants to share ideas on making undergraduate STEM education resilient, adaptable, and equitable.

Moderators:
- Ryan Kelsey, Executive Director, Partnership Development, Markle Foundation, committee member
- Leanne Chukoskie, Director of the Power of NeuroGaming (PoNG) Center, University of California, San Diego, committee member

3:45 Break

4:15 **Access and Inclusion: Beginning with the End in Mind**
How could we redesign the future of STEM learning to increase access, create equity, and leverage community connections?

Panelists:
- Theresa Maldonado, Vice President for Research and Innovation, University of California System
- Yves Salomon-Fernández, President, Greenfield Community College
- Shanika Hope, Principal Amazon Future Engineer, Amazon
- Monica Van, student, University of California, San Diego

Moderator:
Barbara Schaal, Mary Dell Chilton Distinguished Professor, Washington University in St. Louis, committee co-chair

5:15-5:30 **Day One Wrap Up and Preview of Day Two**

- Annette Parker, President, South Central College, committee co-chair
- Barbara Schaal, Mary Dell Chilton Distinguished Professor, Washington University in St. Louis, committee co-chair

<u>Friday, November 13</u>

11:00 ET **Seeds of Innovation: Lessons from Current Innovations in STEM Education**
Current and recent work to reform undergraduate STEM education and ideas for improving equity in the future.

Presenters:
- Karen Marrongelle, Assistant Director for Education and Human Resources, National Science Foundation, Study Sponsor
- Aikaterini (Katerina) Bagiati, Research Scientist, Massachusetts Institute of Technology

Moderators:
- Barbara Schaal, Mary Dell Chilton Distinguished Professor, Washington University in St. Louis, committee co-chair
- Kirk Kolenbrander, Executive Vice President, College of Engineering, Technology, and Aeronautics, Southern New Hampshire University, committee member

11:30 **Fast-Changing Technology: Uses and Ethical Issues**
The role of technology in altering both educational experiences and our larger society, the complexity of issues raised by current and potential changes, and how we as individuals and as a society can make informed decisions about its use.

Panelists:
- Michael Torrence, President, Motlow State Community College
- Sae Schatz, Director, Advanced Distributed Learning
- Nishal Mohan, Founder, mohuman
- Nicole Jackson, Chief Technology Officer, Duet Health

Moderator:
Christine Ortiz, Dean for Graduate Education, Massachusetts Institute of Technology, committee member

12:30 **Challenging Our Strategies and Expectations: What Students Learn, Why, and How**
Which of our current structures best support these goals and which should be rethought?

Panelists:
- Amitava 'Babi' Mitra, Ph.D., Executive Director, New Engineering Education Transformation (NEET), Massachusetts Institute of Technology
- Suzanne Weekes, Associate Dean of Undergraduate Studies, Worcester Polytechnic Institute
- Clarissa Sorensen-Unruh, Professor of Chemistry, Central New Mexico Community College
- Sakereh Carter, Ph.D. Student, Community Engagement, Environmental Justice, and Health, University of Maryland

Moderators:
- Lynn Andrea Stein, Professor of Computer and Cognitive Science, Olin College, committee member
- Monique Umphrey, President, Houston Community College, committee member

1:30 Break

2:00 **A Call to Action: Creating the Future that We Want**
The Future STEM Ecosystem of 2040

Presenter:
Susan Singer, Provost, Rollins College

Panelists:
- Alegra Eroy-Reveles, Assistant Teaching Professor, Chemistry and Biochemistry, University of California, Santa Cruz
- Rufus Glasper, President and CEO, League for Innovation in the Community College
- David Soo, Chief of Staff, Jobs for the Future

Moderator:
Kinnis Gosha, Hortenius I. Chenault Endowed Associate Professor, Department of Computer Science and Director of the Culturally Relevant Computing Lab, Morehouse College, committee member

3:00 **Building on Current Innovations to Create a Vision for the Future**
Participant activity to imagine visions for the future of undergraduate STEM education.

Moderators:
- Cathy Manduca, Director, Science Education Resource Center, Carleton College, committee member
- Lynn Andrea Stein, Professor of Computer and Cognitive Science, Olin College, committee member

4:00 Break

4:30-5:30 **Where Do We Go from Here?**
Next Week and Beyond

- Annette Parker, President, South Central College, committee co-chair
- Barbara Schaal, Mary Dell Chilton Distinguished Professor, Washington University in St. Louis, committee co-chair

November 16-18: Participant activities to expand on visions for the future of undergraduate STEM education and to revisit earlier discussion topics.

<u>Thursday, November 19</u>

1:00 ET **Returning to the Present, Creating the Future**
Working together to drive local and national change.

- Annette Parker, President, South Central College, committee co-chair
- Barbara Schaal, Mary Dell Chilton Distinguished Professor, Washington University in St. Louis, committee co-chair

1:15 **Redesigning Campuses, Classrooms, and Learning Experiences**
Creating more accessible and successful student experiences for 2040.

Panelists:
- Pam Eddinger, President, Bunker Hill Community College
- Amber Luther, Planner and Senior Associate, Populous
- Annmarie Caño, Dean of the College of Arts and Sciences, Gonzaga University
- Michael Roberts, Founder and CEO, San Diego Code School

Moderators:
- Nicholas Horton, Beitzel Professor in Technology and Society (Statistics and Data Science), Amherst College, committee member
- Leanne Chukoskie, Director of the Power of NeuroGaming (PoNG) Center, University of California, San Diego, committee member

2:00 **New Learning Pathways**
Participant activity on designing flexible, personal, problem-focused, and lifelong learning experiences.

Moderators:
- Leanne Chukoskie, Director of the Power of NeuroGaming (PoNG) Center, University of California, San Diego, committee member
- Nicholas Horton, Beitzel Professor in Technology and Society (Statistics and Data Science), Amherst College, committee member

3:00 Break

3:30 **Sharing Symposium Learning and Action Items for Change**

Catalyzing innovations on our campuses and through our networks and soliciting participant input on NSF-sponsored activities to share insights from the symposium throughout 2021.

Moderator:

Ryan Kelsey, Executive Director, Partnership Development, Markle Foundation, committee member

4:15-4:30 **Reflections and Closing Remarks**

- Robin Wright, Division Director, Division on Undergraduate Education, National Science Foundation, Study Sponsor
- Annette Parker, President, South Central College, committee co-chair
- Barbara Schaal, Mary Dell Chilton Distinguished Professor, Washington University in St. Louis, committee co-chair

Appendix C

Biographical Sketches of Symposium Speakers and Moderators

Annette Parker (*Committee Co-chair*) is the president of South Central College, a Minnesota state community and technical college. She has been involved in manufacturing industry and workforce education for more than 35 years. She started her career at General Motors in Lansing, Michigan, and moved into education first as a faculty member and administrator at Lansing Community College and later as system director of workforce education for the Kentucky Community and Technical College System. Parker has served on President Obama's Advanced Manufacturing Partnership (AMP) Steering Committee 2.0 and co-chaired AMP's Demand-Driven Workforce Development work team. She currently serves on the Center for Community College Student Engagement National Advisory Board, Council for Adult and Experiential Learning Advisory Council (Chair), NASEM Roundtable on Systemic Change in Undergraduate STEM Education, The Presidents' Roundtable (vice convenor) and Iowa-Minnesota Campus Compact Board of Directors, and MIT's Work of the Future Task Force. She earned an A.A.S. in industrial drafting from Lansing Community College, a B.S. in technical education and an M.S. in career and technical education from Ferris State University, and an Ed.D. in educational leadership from Western Kentucky University.

Barbara Schaal (*Committee Co-chair*) is the Mary Dell Chilton distinguished professor at the Washington University in St. Louis and is a nationally recognized plant evolutionary biologist who uses DNA sequences to understand evolutionary processes. She was among the first plant scientists to use molecular biology-based approaches to understand evolutionary processes in plants, and she has worked to advance understanding of plant molecular systematics and population genetics. Schaal has been president of the Botanical Society of America, the Society for the Study of Evolution, and the American Association for the Advancement of Science. She is an elected member of the American Academy of Arts and Sciences and National Academy of Sciences, where she served as vice president for 8 years. She was appointed as a U.S. science envoy by former Secretary of State Hillary Clinton. Schaal has served as chair of the Division on Earth and Life Studies at the National Research Council and was a member of President Obama's Council of Advisors for Science and Technology from 2009 to 2017. In 2019, she received the National Science Board's Public Service Medal and joined the board of directors of the Supporters of Agricultural Research Foundation. From 2013 to 2020, she served as dean of the faculty of arts and sciences where she oversaw all academic, financial, and administration aspects. Schaal graduated from the University of Illinois, Chicago, with a degree in biology, and received her Ph.D. from Yale University.

Marcia McNutt is a geophysicist and the 22nd president of the National Academy of Sciences. From 2013 to 2016, she was editor-in-chief of *Science*. She was director of the U.S. Geological Survey (USGS) from 2009 to 2013, during which time USGS responded to a number of major disasters, including the Deepwater Horizon oil spill. For her work to help contain that spill, McNutt was awarded the U.S. Coast Guard's Meritorious Service Medal. She is a fellow of the American Geophysical Union (AGU), Geological Society of America, American Association for the Advancement of Science, and the International Association of Geodesy. McNutt is a member of the American Philosophical Society and the American Academy of Arts and Sciences, and a foreign member of the Royal Society, UK, the Russian Academy of Sciences, and the Chinese Academy of Sciences. In 1998, she was awarded the AGU's Macelwane Medal for research accomplishments by a young scientist, and she received the Maurice Ewing Medal in 2007 for her contributions to deep-sea exploration. McNutt received a B.A. in physics from Colorado College and her Ph.D. in earth sciences from Scripps Institution of Oceanography.

Aikaterini (Katerina) Bagiati is currently a research scientist at the MIT Office of Open Learning. She is actively involved in the development and the assessment related to MIT's national and international educational projects and collaborations and conducts research at the preK–12 and higher-education levels, in the efficacy of innovative learning mechanisms and pedagogical approaches used in initiatives mentioned above. Her research interests are in the areas of early engineering, educational technologies, STEM curriculum development and teacher training, and design-based learning. She first worked as a software engineer, and later as a computer science and technology teacher in middle and high school classes, while in parallel participated in numerous K–12 STEM summer camps. She received a diploma in electrical and computer engineering and a master's degree in advanced digital communication systems from Aristotle University in Thessaloniki, Greece. In 2008, she was one of the first graduate students to join the pioneer School of Engineering Education at Purdue University. In 2011, she acquired her doctorate in engineering education, followed by a postdoctoral associate appointment within the MIT-SUTD Collaboration at MIT.

Annmarie Caño is a professor of psychology and dean of the College of Arts and Sciences at Gonzaga University. Her research has focused on the role of empathy and perspective-taking on individual and relationship well-being for a variety of dyads, including couples facing chronic illness, parents and children with illness, and also adjudicated adolescents. In recognition of her research contributions, she was elected in 2016 as a fellow of the American Psychological Association. Her administrative work has included recruitment and retention efforts to prepare students and faculty from diverse backgrounds for academic, professional, and personal success. She has conducted research on holistic review in graduate admissions and launched a competency-based professional development initiative that uses microcredentials to recognize graduate students' achievements. Caño is a first-generation college student. She earned her master's and doctoral degrees in psychology from Stony Brook University and her bachelor's degree in psychology from Princeton University.

Sakereh Carter is currently pursuing her Ph.D. in environmental health sciences at the University of Maryland in the Community Engagement, Environmental Justice, and Health Lab. Her research focuses on environmental justice across the U.S. Gulf and East Coast. More specifically, the goal is to empower communities through a community-based participatory research framework/citizen science and educational outreach and influence policy directives with evidence-based research. Carter received her B.S. in animal biology and her M.A. in biological sciences.

Erin A. Cech is an assistant professor of sociology at the University of Michigan. Her research examines how inequality is reproduced through processes that are built into seemingly innocuous cultural beliefs and practices. She uses quantitative and qualitative approaches to examine inequality in STEM professions, examines how cultural definitions of "good work" and "good workers" can anchor inequality in the workforce, and studies how cultural understandings of the extent and origin of inequality help to uphold unequal social structures. She received her Ph.D. in sociology at the University of California, San Diego.

Vicki Chandler is the provost and chief academic officer at Minerva Schools at Keck Graduate Institute. Prior to Minerva, she served as the chief program officer for science at the Gordon and Betty Moore Foundation, while also teaching at the University of Oregon and the University of Arizona. She is recognized as one of the foremost geneticists in the world, having conducted critical research in the field of plant genetics for more than three decades. In 2014, she was appointed to the National Science Board by President Barack Obama for a 6-year term. She is passionate about helping students develop the skills they need to be successful in their future careers, part of which is directing them to be curious, lifelong learners. Chandler was a postdoctoral fellow at Stanford University, received her B.A. from the University of California, Berkeley, and received her Ph.D. from the University of California, San Francisco.

Leanne Chukoskie is the associate director for the Research on Autism and Development Laboratory and also the director of the Power of NeuroGaming (PoNG) Center at the University of California, San Diego. Her current research focuses on sensory-motor behavior, especially eye movement behavior and its neural correlates across both typical and atypical development. This focus has evolved from early studies of basic visual and eye movement processes combined with an interest and experience working with individuals on the autism spectrum. She seeks ways to use sensor-based technology to create closed-loop adaptive systems for intervention and assessments to evaluate intervention outcomes efficacy. Chukoskie and her collaborator have designed and delivered a suite of gaze-contingent training games to improve spatial re-orientation of attention and gaze control of teens on the autism spectrum. This work led to the creation of the PoNG Center to develop and test sensor-enabled games targeted for different cognitive and motor skill assessment or improvement. This work also led to the creation of BrainLeap Technologies, a company that seeks to make attention training games broadly available. Chukoskie also has more than 10 years of experience in the science of learning through her participation in the National Science Foundation-funded Temporal Dynamics of Learning Center and her use of innovative active learning methods honed while teaching at Minerva Schools. She earned her B.A. in neural science and anthropology from the University of Pennsylvania in Philadelphia and a Ph.D. in neuroscience from New York University.

F. Fleming Crim has a distinguished record of accomplishments in research and education, including serving as the chief operating officer for the

National Science Foundation (NSF) since 2018. He spent 40 years in the Department of Chemistry at the University of Wisconsin–Madison, where he is now the John E. Willard and Hilldale professor emeritus. From 2013 to 2017, Crim served as NSF's assistant director for mathematical and physical sciences. He has lectured around the world and published more than 150 papers leading to awards such as the Plyler Prize of the American Physical Society, the Langmuir Award of the American Chemical Society, and the Centenary Medal of the Royal Society of Chemistry (London). He is a fellow of the American Physical Society, American Chemical Society, and the American Association for the Advancement of Science. He is a member of both the National Academy of Sciences and the American Academy of Arts and Sciences. Crim received his bachelor's degree from Southwestern University and his doctorate from Cornell University.

Alegra Eroy-Reveles is an assistant teaching professor of chemistry and biochemistry at the University of California, Santa Cruz. As an innovative, community-based chemistry professor, her purpose is to prepare a diverse cadre of STEM graduates by translating her research findings into higher-education practices. Eroy-Reveles has a B.S. in Spanish and a B.S. and Ph.D. in chemistry.

Rufus Glasper is president and chief executive officer of the League for Innovation in the Community College, an international nonprofit organization that strives to cultivate innovation in the Community College space, advance the community college field, and make a positive difference for students and communities. He is the chancellor emeritus of the Maricopa Community Colleges, one of the nation's largest multicollege community college systems. He served as chancellor from 2003 to February 2016 and held district leadership positions for three decades. Nationally, Glasper serves as an advisory board member for the Center for Community College Student Engagement, the University of Texas at Austin; Community College Research Center, Teachers College, Columbia University; and The Belk Center for Community College Leadership and Research, North Carolina State University. He serves on the board of directors for the Education Design Lab and COMAP, the Consortium for Mathematics and Its Applications. Glasper earned a bachelor's degree in business administration from Luther College (Decorah, Iowa) and a master's and advanced degrees in school business administration from Northern Illinois University. He received his Ph.D. in higher-education finance from the University of Arizona.

Kinnis Gosha (Go-Shay) is the Hortenius I. Chenault endowed associate professor in the Department of Computer Science and the director of the Culturally Relevant Computing Lab at Morehouse College. His primary research interests include expanding computer science education, broadening participation in computing, green computing, and culturally relevant computing. Undergraduate researchers in his lab, the Culturally Relevant Computing Lab, investigate research problems centered on creating innovative computing technologies to solve cultural problems and issues. Applications of his research include robotics, avatars, and video games. He owns Gosha Technologies, a website development company. He received his Ph.D. in human-centered computing from Clemson University and was the inaugural graduate for the program, as well as the first African American to obtain a doctoral degree in human-centered computing. He also holds an M.S. from Auburn University and a B.S. from Albany State University.

Shanika Hope is a former elementary school teacher, principal and high school turnaround specialist with more than 25 years of experience in education. She has managed and/or supported more than 36 DC public schools and public charter schools in various capacities. Prior to her current role as head of the Amazon Future Engineer Program at Amazon, her previous roles include head of content and research at Amazon Web Services; vice president of national urban markets initiatives at McGraw Hill Education; vice president of curriculum and instruction at Discovery Education; and assistant superintendent of elementary and secondary education for the Washington, DC, State Education Office. She also served as a school principal and teacher in both Washington, DC, and Virginia. Hope earned a Ph.D. in education leadership and a master's degree in math and science education from Old Dominion University, where she was selected as a Holmes Scholar.

Nicholas Horton is Beitzel professor of technology and society and professor of statistics at Amherst College. He is an applied biostatistician whose work is based squarely within the mathematical and computational sciences but spans other fields in order to ensure that biomedical research is conducted on a sound footing. He has published more than 170 papers in the statistics and biomedical literature and four books on statistical computing and data science. He has taught a variety of courses in statistics and related fields, including introductory statistics, data science, probability, theoretical statistics, regression, and design of experiments. He is passionate about improving quantitative and computational literacy for students with a variety of backgrounds as well as engagement and mastery of higher-level concepts and capacities to think with data. Horton received the American Statistical Association (ASA) Waller Award for Distinguished Teaching, the Mathematical Association of America Hogg Award for Excellence in Teaching, the

Mu Sigma Rho Statistics Education Award, and the ASA Founders Award. He was a co-principal investigator of the National Science Foundation-funded Project MOSAIC, serves as the chair of the Committee of Presidents of Statistical Societies, is a fellow of the ASA and the American Association for the Advancement of Science, and was a research fellow at the Bureau of Labor Statistics. Horton earned an A.B. from Harvard College and a Sc.D. in biostatistics from the Harvard T.H. Chan School of Public Health.

Nicole Jackson is the chief technology officer at Duet Health and serves as an American Association for the Advancement of Science IF/THEN Ambassador. She is pursuing a graduate degree in education at Drexel University. Her research focuses on the application of research in technology to improve performance outcomes using mobile and web applications that aim to improve task achievement and contextual retention. Jackson obtained her B.A. in interdisciplinary studies and an M.S. in creativity and innovation technology.

Ryan Kelsey leads the Markle Foundation's partnership strategy across all of its philanthropic initiatives as the executive director of partnership development. He weaves together innovation, philanthropy, nonprofit leadership, network strategies, and partnerships to work for a more equitable world. The primary vehicle for conducting his work has been to foster the improvement of educational systems to accelerate upward social mobility for historically disadvantaged populations, but his previous experiences also cross over into public health, the environment, and other sectors. Kelsey is also a member of the Board of Advisors for Project Kaleidoscope and a board member for the Black Rock Forest Consortium. He received his B.S. in biology from Santa Clara University, and his M.A. and Ed.D. in communications and education from Columbia University.

Kirk Kolenbrander is executive vice president, College of Engineering, Technology, and Aeronautics at Southern New Hampshire University (SNHU). He is leading the construction of a new innovative building on the main campus that will feature a makerspace, a 3D printing room, a drone flying area and unmanned aerial vehicle prep space, and a robotics lab. He is committed to helping SNHU to create a new, scalable model for higher education and wants to create a sustainable model that provides affordable, engaging learning experiences that help produce employees ready to contribute to companies. Prior to joining SNHU, he was a faculty member at MIT, where he won the MIT Baker Award for Faculty Excellence in Undergraduate Teaching and the MIT Smith Award for Outstanding Faculty Contributions to Student Life. Kolenbrander led the creation of MIT LeaderShape, an intensive leadership curriculum he has taught during

Independent Activities Period for nearly 25 years, providing more than 1,000 MIT students with a formative experience in community-centered problem solving. He was instrumental in forging a new partnership between the Institute and the MIT Alumni Association. He has also led efforts to introduce changes intended to enhance diversity and inclusion at MIT, including improvements related to orientation for incoming students, mental health services, implicit bias training, financial aid, and student surveys and data collection. Kolenbrander holds a Ph.D. in physical chemistry from the University of Illinois at Urbana-Champaign.

Arthur Lee is Chevron fellow and principal advisor, environment and climate change, at Chevron Services Company, based in San Ramon, California. He has held positions of increasing responsibilities, including the corporation-wide formulation of strategic positioning and policy development on issues ranging from Chevron's internal energy policy, U.S. air pollution issues, to actions addressing climate change concerns. He was appointed by the U.S. Secretary of Commerce to the National Climate Assessment Development and Advisory Committee, responsible for the next assessment of climate change impacts on the United States. Lee is team leader on deployment issues in the CO_2 Capture Project, which is the global joint industry-government project to develop the next generation of CO_2 capture and storage technology. From April 2005 to May 2007, he served as the chairman of the Climate Change Working Group of the International Petroleum Industry Environmental Conservation Association. Lee served as the review editor of the International Panel on Climate Change's (IPCC) special report *Carbon Dioxide Capture and Storage* (2005). The IPCC shared the 2007 Nobel Peace Prize. In August 2006 and November 2007, with his leadership, Chevron was the key sponsor of the series of G8/International Energy Agency/Carbon Sequestration Leadership Workshop on Carbon Capture and Storage. The workshop series was successful in generating a consensus on recommendations for near-term opportunities for carbon capture and storage. These recommendations were delivered to G8 leaders.

Amber Luther is a planner and senior associate at Populous. Her work focuses on innovative urban designs and planning, which requires working alongside many city governments and universities to plan and construct large-scale projects. Luther received her B.S. in architecture and multimedia.

Lindsey Malcom-Piqueux is the senior institutional research analyst at Caltech. Her primary interest centers on postsecondary access and success for minoritized women and men in STEM fields. She has conducted research in several areas including the relationship between financial aid and STEM outcomes, the role of 4-year Minority-Serving Institutions and

Community Colleges in creating educational equity in STEM, and gender equity in STEM among minoritized populations. Malcom-Piqueux also studies the educational experiences and outcomes of students of color at Historically Black Colleges and Universities, predominantly Black institutions, Hispanic-Serving Institutions, and tribal colleges and examines the congruence of the minority-serving designation and academic outcomes among their target populations. Her work has appeared in *Educational Researcher*, *The Review of Higher Education*, *Harvard Educational Review*, among other journals, and in volumes edited by Routledge, SUNY Press, Johns Hopkins University Press, and Stylus Publishing. Malcom-Piqueux received her M.S. and S.B. in planetary science from Caltech and MIT, respectively, and her Ph.D. in urban education with an emphasis on higher education from the University of Southern California.

Theresa A. Maldonado is the vice president for research and innovation for the University of California system. She has extensive experience at the federal level in advancing engineering research, education, and commercialization initiatives. From 2011 to 2014, she served as a division director in the Engineering Directorate at the National Science Foundation (NSF). She was responsible for support of interdisciplinary research centers, research translation, innovations in engineering education, special initiatives in support of military veterans, broadening participation in engineering, and workforce development programs. Her initial appointment at NSF was from 1999 to 2001, when she served as a program director in the Engineering Research Centers Program and represented the Engineering Directorate on several NSF-wide committees. Before entering academia, she was a member of technical staff at AT&T Bell Laboratories working on optical fiber components and systems. Maldonado is a registered professional engineer in Texas. She earned Ph.D., M.S.E.E., and B.E.E. with Highest Honors degrees in electrical engineering, all from the Georgia Institute of Technology.

Cathy Manduca is director of the Science Education Resource Center at Carleton College, where she leads work to improve education guiding projects to completion, developing new directions, raising funds, and managing staff. This work supports communities of educators in learning together and collaborating to create resources supporting widespread improvement in various aspects of education. Her research focuses on understanding faculty learning and the impact of professional networks on educational practice. Manduca was the executive director of the National Association of Geoscience Teachers from 2007 to 2019. She serves on the Board on Science Education and the LabX Advisory Board of the National Academies of Sciences, Engineering, and Medicine, and has served on the elected leadership for the American Geophysical Union and American Association for the

Advancement of Science (AAAS) Education Section in the past. She is a fellow of AAAS and the Geological Society of America, and past recipient of the American Geophysical Union's award for Excellence in Earth and Space Education. Manduca received her B.A. in geology from Williams College and her Ph.D. in geology from the California Institute of Technology.

Karen Marrongelle serves as the assistant director of the Directorate for Education and Human Resources at the National Science Foundation (NSF). Her career as a leader in the research community has been marked by a deep commitment to diversity, equity, and inclusion. As an administrator, she has focused on understanding the causes of disparities in educational opportunities and establishing strategic visions for addressing those issues. She served as dean of the College of Liberal Arts and Sciences at Portland State University, where she worked to implement student inclusivity measures, establish public-private partnerships to support research, and optimize the school's use of grants from NSF and other funding organizations. In addition to her work as dean, she served as a professor of mathematics and statistics at Portland State University beginning in 2001. Prior to her appointment as dean, she held positions as the vice chancellor for academic strategies and assistant vice chancellor for academic standards and collaboration with the Oregon University System. Marrongelle has a bachelor's degree in mathematics and philosophy from Albright College, a master's degree in mathematics from Lehigh University, and a doctorate in mathematics education from the University of New Hampshire.

Tonya M. Matthews is the director of STEM learning innovation and associate provost for inclusive workforce development at Wayne State University, and a thought leader in STEM education and engagement, organizational equity and inclusion, and informal, community-driven learning. She is noted for her skill in bringing diverse voices into common conversation and has been recognized by *Crain's Business* as one of Michigan's 100 Most Influential Women. She is currently vice-chair for the National Assessment Governing Board (which defines the Nation's Report Card in math and science) and she is a member of the National Academies of Sciences, Engineering, and Medicine's Board on Science Education. She is the recipient of a Whitaker Foundation Award for Engineering Excellence and an alumni member of National Society of Black Engineers and Society for Women Engineers. As a community-driven science education and community-engaged science advocate, Matthews founded The STEMinista Project, an initiative supporting middle school girls in exploring tools and careers in STEM. The program uses collective impact program design, engages a global role model database, and works with partners to open access to 1,000+ hours of STEM experiences for participants every year. Previously, she was president and chief executive officer of Michigan Science Center and led its climb to becoming the STEM Hub for greater Detroit and the state of Michigan. During her tenure, Matthews positioned the center and Detroit as an epicenter of STEM and garnered national recognition by hosting critical convenings such as the release of the first Nation's Report Card on Technology and Engineering Literacy. Matthews received her B.S.E. in biomedical and electrical engineering from Duke University and her Ph.D. in biomedical engineering from Johns Hopkins University.

Amitava "Babi" Mitra is the founding executive director, New Engineering Education Transformation, MIT. He is co-leading a program to reimagine and transform MIT's undergraduate engineering education, arguably one of the most impactful initiatives in higher education today. He has more than 25 years of experience in institution building, higher education, corporate e-learning, and distance education. He transformed a small e-learning research and development group into the profitable Knowledge Solutions Business. He was a founding member of the Pan-Himalayan Grassroots Development Foundation, a nongovernmental organization established 25 years ago in the Kumaon Mountains. He was the founding dean for the School of Engineering & Technology, BML Munjal University, India, where he launched Joy of Engineering, a first-year hands-on course designed to get students engaged with engineering. He was the first chief of the Distance Learning Programs Unit at Birla Institute of Technology and Science (BITS), Pilani, India. Mitra received his Ph.D. in chemical engineering from BITS.

Mark Mitsui is the president of Portland Community College (PCC), the first Asian American president in the 58-year history of PCC, which educates more than 60,000 students annually and is the largest higher-education institution in the state of Oregon. He was selected by the *Portland Business Journal* as an executive of the year in 2018 and currently serves on several boards, which include the Governor's Workforce and Talent Development Board, the Portland Business Alliance Board, and the Greater Portland Incorporated Board, the Higher Education Steering Council for Second Nature, We Are Still In, American Council on Education, and the President's Advisory Council for Phi Theta Kappa. Prior to working at PCC, he served in the Obama administration as the deputy assistant secretary for community colleges in the U.S. Department of Education. In this role, he advanced the President's and department's Community College agenda through strategic partnerships across federal agencies and with national stakeholders. He also served as president of North Seattle College, vice president of student services at South Seattle College, assistant dean of student services at Green River Community College (where he was awarded an Exemplary Leadership Award by the Chair Academy), and director of student success at North Seattle College. He entered into the community and technical college arena as a teacher at Renton Technical College, where he was awarded an Outstanding Faculty Award in 1994. Mitsui holds a bachelor's degree in physical education from Western Washington University and completed a master's degree in education at the University of Washington.

Nishal Mohan founded the 501c(3) nonprofit organization, mohuman, in 2018. Through self-determination, education, multidisciplinary experience, and deep social good ideals, he has worked in the nonprofit, startup, city, and federal sectors to blend science, technology, policy, and social justice for creative undertakings that serve all people. He is a fierce advocate, strategist, educator, and doer devoted to empowering those underserved by society to have an easier path to social, intellectual, and economic equity in their communities. Mohan received his B.A. in biology and his Ph.D. in molecular biology.

Anne Marie Núñez is a professor of educational studies in the Higher Education and Student Affairs Program at The Ohio State University. Her award-winning research employs sociological approaches to advance equitable postsecondary educational opportunities for historically underserved groups in higher education. Her scholarship has focused on (1) postsecondary trajectories of Latinx, first-generation, migrant, and English Learner students; (2) institutional diversity in the United States, including the role of Hispanic-Serving Institutions (HSIs) in promoting college opportunities; and (3) building inclusive and equitable environments in STEM disciplines and HSIs. She co-edited *Hispanic-Serving Institutions: Advancing Research and Transformative Practice*, an International Latino Book Award winner that is the first book to focus on HSIs as organizations and their role in the American higher-education system. She has served as a National Academy of Sciences, Engineering, and Medicine committee member, helping to co-author and disseminate a 2019 report on the contributions of minority-serving institutions to the science workforce titled *Minority Serving Institutions: America's Underutilized Resource for Strengthening the STEM Workforce*. Her current research is funded by more than $10 million in grants from the National Science Foundation to build equitable environments in geosciences and computing, raise Latinx attainment in STEM fields, and strengthen STEM capacity in HSIs. Núñez received an A.B. from Harvard University, an M.A. from Stanford University School of Education, and her M.A. and Ph.D. in higher education and organizational change from the University of California, Los Angeles Graduate School of Education.

Eloy Oakley is the chancellor of the California Community College system. His career in education includes serving as an adjunct faculty member teaching in and coordinating the Environmental Technology Certificate Program at Golden West College, manager of risk services at the Coast Community College District, vice president of college services at Oxnard College, and assistant superintendent/executive vice president of administrative services at the Long Beach Community College District. In 2007, he was appointed superintendent-president of the Long Beach Community College District, one of the most diverse Community Colleges in the nation, and he became increasingly well-known for providing statewide and national leadership on improving educational outcomes of historically underrepresented students. Partnering with the Long Beach Unified School District and Cal State Long Beach, Oakley helped form the nationally recognized Long Beach College Promise, a program creating clear, structured pathways for students to move from high school to Long Beach Community College and onto Cal State Long Beach. The James Irvine Foundation recognized him with its Leadership Award in 2014, the same year he was appointed chancellor to the University of California's Board of Regents. In 2015, President Obama launched the America's College Promise initiative that was modeled in part on the Long Beach Promise. Oakley earned his bachelor's degree in environmental analysis and design and a master's degree in business administration from the University of California, Irvine.

Christine Ortiz is Morris Cohen professor of materials science and engineering at MIT and the founder and inaugural philanthropic benefactor of a new nonprofit higher-education institution, Station1 (http://www.station1.org), that is building a new model of postsecondary education through an inclusive, integrated, interdisciplinary approach to socially directed science and technology education, research, and entrepreneurship. Ortiz has been active in shaping the national and international dialog on higher education and has spoken at the National Science Foundation; the National Institutes of Health; the National Academies of Sciences, Engineering, and Medicine; the United Nations; the League of European Research Universities (a network of 23 leading European research universities); Semesp (a national organization for Brazilian higher education); and the American Association for Colleges and Universities, among many other venues. She is a distinguished scientist and engineer with more than 175 scholarly publications, has supervised the research projects of more than 100 students from 10 different academic disciplines, and received 30 national and international honors, including the Presidential Early-Career Award in Science and Engineering. Ortiz obtained her B.S. from Rensselaer Polytechnic Institute and her M.S. and Ph.D. from Cornell University, all in the field of materials science and engineering, with a minor in theoretical and applied mechanics.

Michael Roberts is the founder of San Diego Code School. He has worn many hats from software engineer to chief executive officer. He is a board member of San Diego JavaScript Community. He is a Fullstack JavaScript practitioner with more than 30 years of experience coding. He has helped launch more than 100 student careers and has graduates working at IBM/RedHat, Apple, WalmartLabs, Sony, AWS, and many tech companies.

Josipa Roksa currently serves as director of strategic academic programs and professor of sociology and education at the University of Virginia. Her current research focuses on understanding the experiences and outcomes of first-generation and low-income students, and more broadly the role of socioeconomic status in shaping students' trajectories through both undergraduate and graduate education. The central question guiding her scholarly inquiry is: To what extent does education amplify, preserve, or reduce social inequality? To answer the question, she is examining how students' experiences vary by race and ethnicity, particularly in STEM fields. Current projects are charting coursework trajectories, considering the role of family support, and exploring students' interactions with faculty and peers, all with the goal of understanding the mechanisms that generate social inequality. In her earlier work, she has explored inequalities in learning (and specifically development of critical-thinking skills in college) and K–12 education. Roksa received a B.A. in psychology from Mount Holyoke College and a Ph.D. in sociology from New York University.

Yves Salomon-Fernández is president of Greenfield Community College. She previously served as president of Cumberland County College in New Jersey and interim president of MassBay Community College. In her career in higher education, Salomon-Fernández has served at large and medium-sized selective private and public universities, as well as open-access colleges in urban, suburban, and rural settings in the United States. Internationally, Salomon-Fernández has served with the United Nations in Mexico and as a consultant for the Bermuda Ministry of Education. She is a recognized thought leader, writing and speaking on issues related to reinventing higher education, rural innovation, equity, and women's leadership. In 2018, *Diverse Issues in Higher Education* named Salomon-Fernández one of the Top 25 Women in Higher Education. She is a member of the American Association of Community College's Commission on Small and Rural Colleges and serves on Jobs for the Future's Policy Leadership Trust. She is also a member of the Federal Reserve Bank of Boston's Community Development Council. She advocates for a greater role of the liberal arts as a board member at Mass Humanities. She also has a keen interest in the effect of the opioids epidemic on rural communities. Salomon-Fernández emigrated with her family from Haiti and is a graduate of Boston Latin School. She received her undergraduate degree from the University of Massachusetts, Boston and holds a certificate from the University of Oxford. Her master's degree is from the London School of Economics and her Ph.D. from Boston College.

Sae Schatz emphasizes advocacy for learning science as director of the Advance Distributed Learning (ADL) Initiative. Prior to joining the ADL Initiative, Schatz was a senior consultant with Executive Development Associates, and before that she was the chief scientist for MESH Solutions, LLC (a DSCI Company) in Orlando, Florida. She has worked on a number of well-known projects including the Marine Corps' Making Good Instructors Great effort, the National Transportation Safety Administration award-winning Border Hunter research and instructional design project, and the Joint Staff (J7)'s Blended Learning–Training System. She served on the University of Central Florida faculty from 2006 to 2011 (teaching courses in human-systems integration, visual and web design, and web development) and continues to support the Modeling and Simulation Graduate Program as an occasional adjunct instructor. Schatz received her Ph.D. in modeling and simulation from the University of Central Florida.

Wanda Sigur is as an aerospace consultant for both emerging space exploration companies and traditional aerospace industry companies, continuing her lifelong commitment to the success of aerospace missions, the growth of the aerospace profession, and new technology implementation. She retired from Lockheed Martin as vice president and general manager of the Civil Space business where she had executive responsibility for national space programs relating to human space flight and space science missions, including planetary, solar, astrophysical, and Earth remote sensing for civil government agencies. These major programs included the Orion Multi-purpose Crew Vehicle, Hubble and Spitzer space telescopes, GOES-R weather satellites, Juno, GRAIL, MAVEN, Mars Reconnaissance Orbiter, Mars Odyssey, and OSIRIS-REx planetary missions, and the company's nuclear space power programs. Sigur's key experience reflects her passion for growing an inclusive and progressive space exploration environment. As president and founder of Lambent Engineering LLC, she currently provides support in strategic planning, program review, and program management disciplines as well as sharing historical performance on NASA programs. In addition, she serves on boards of advisors of emerging space exploration companies and nonprofits and helps push key technologies to mature implementations. She is a member of the National Academy of Engineering and the Academy of Medicine, Engineering, and Science of Texas. She is a member of the National Academies of Sciences, Engineering, and Medicine's Aeronautics and Space Evaluation Board (ASEB) and chair of the ASEB Space Technology Industry Government University Roundtable. Sigur received her B.S.

in materials engineering from Rice University and her M.B.A. from Tulane University.

Susan Singer is the vice president for academic affairs and provost at Rollins College and a professor in the Department of Biology. Immediately prior to joining Rollins, she was the director for the Division of Undergraduate Education at the National Science Foundation and coordinated 14 federal agencies in implementing the undergraduate strategic objectives of the first Federal STEM Education 5-Year Strategic Plan. Previously, she served as the Laurence McKinley Gould professor, in the Departments of Biology and Cognitive Science at Carleton College for 30 years, where she had the opportunity to direct the Perlman Center for Learning and Teaching. She is an American Association for the Advancement of Science fellow and received the American Society of Plant Biology Teaching Award and Botanical Society of America Charles Bessey Award. She served on numerous boards, including the National Science Foundation Education and Human Resources Advisory Committee, and is the current chair of the National Academies of Sciences, Engineering, and Medicine's Board on Science Education. Singer received her B.S., M.S., and Ph.D., all from Rensselaer Polytechnic Institute.

David Soo is chief of staff for Jobs for the Future (JFF) and provides strategic and programmatic leadership for key initiatives across JFF and JFF Labs. His work includes the design, development, and incubation of initiatives supporting JFF's mission of accelerating the alignment and transformation of the American workforce and education systems to ensure access to economic advancement for all. Before joining JFF, Soo spent more than 7 years as a senior policy advisor at the U.S. Department of Education. He was a key architect of the department's higher-education innovation agenda during the Obama administration and later served in the Office of the Secretary's Office of Educational Technology. Some key policies and projects he worked on yielded new and refreshed federal initiatives, including the EQUIP pilot program, the First in the World Grant Program, and the Higher Ed Ecosystem Challenge. He also led a series of meetings convened by the U.S. Department of Education and the Obama White House to promote innovation. Soo has appeared on NPR, the PBS News Hour, and Federal News Radio, and he has been quoted by *Inside Higher Ed* and *U.S. News & World Report*. He has spoken at events at the White House, the Aspen Institute, the National Academies of Sciences, Engineering, and Medicine, ASU+GSV Summit, SXSW EDU, Educause, the American Association of Colleges and Universities, and LearnLaunch. He is also a senior scholar at Georgetown University's Center for New Designs in Learning.

Clarissa Sorensen-Unruh is a full-time chemistry instructor at Central New Mexico Community College in Albuquerque, New Mexico. She is also a dual degree graduate student (M.S. in statistics and Ph.D. in learning sciences at the University of New Mexico [UNM]), where she is also listed as adjunct faculty for the Department of Chemistry and Chemical Biology. She currently serves on the communication advisory board on the UNM ADVANCE grant, as an educational collaborator on the National Science Foundation (NSF) CAREER grant, as a regular reviewer for NSF grants, and served from 2014 to 2016 as the Central New Mexico subaward principal investigator for the National Institutes of Health IRACDA UNM ASERT. Her first book, *Communicating Chemistry through Social Media*, on which she serves as both the main editor and a chapter writer, was published in 2018. She serves as a buddy (virtual and onsite) and an active member of Virtually Connecting, and she also serves in several roles in the American Chemical Society's Division of Chemical Education: social media subgroup chair for the Biennial Conference Committee, a board associate for the Board of Publications, and as chair of the Strategic Task Force for PR. Sorensen-Unruh received an M.S. in statistics and a Ph.D. focused on the learning sciences from the University of New Mexico.

Lynn Andrea Stein is professor of computer and cognitive science at the Olin College of Engineering. From 1990 to 2000, she was an assistant and then associate professor in the Department of Electrical Engineering and Computer Science at MIT and at the AI Laboratory and Laboratory for Computer Science. Her research spans the fields of artificial intelligence, programming languages, and engineering and computer science education. She is a frequent speaker at educational conferences on work including pioneering curricular applications of inexpensive robotics and a curriculum for introductory computer science. Stein has received the National Science Foundation Young Investigator Award, a Bunting fellowship, and several educational awards. She has also served on the executive council of the Association for the Advancement of Artificial Intelligence, on the member services board of the Association for Computing Machinery, and in various leadership positions as a woman in computing. Over the past two and a half decades, Stein has worked with the worldwide community to develop broader visions of computing and engineering education, running educational workshops, leading professional initiatives, and serving on advisory and visiting committees to a wide range of academic institutions and curricular programs. As a member of Olin College's founding faculty, she played a leadership role in many aspects of the development of the college. In 2009, she was named the founding director of Olin's Initiative for Innovation in Engineering Education. Stein has a bachelor's degree, cum laude, in computer science from Harvard and Radcliffe Colleges and master's and doctorate degrees in computer science from Brown University.

Francis Su is the Benediktsson-Karwa professor of mathematics at Harvey Mudd College and a former president of the Mathematical Association of America. In addition to his research in geometric combinatorics, he has written extensively about the dignity of human beings and the wonder of mathematical teaching. In 2013, he received the Haimo Award, a nationwide teaching prize for college math faculty, and in 2018 he won the Halmos-Ford writing award. His work has been featured in *Quanta*, *Wired*, and *The New York Times*. His book *Mathematics for Human Flourishing* (2020) is an inclusive vision of what math is, who it is for, and why anyone should learn it. Su received his Ph.D. from Harvard University.

Vicente Talanquer is a distinguished professor at the University of Arizona. His research centers on the study, reflection, and improvement of chemistry education and science teacher preparation. In particular, his research is directed at characterizing the conceptual frameworks and the patterns of reasoning used by chemistry students to answer questions and solve problems that require qualitative reasoning (e.g., classification, prediction, inference, comparison). He explores how students' ideas and reasoning strategies evolve as they develop more expertise in the discipline (trajectories of expertise). These studies are of central importance not only to design learning progressions that foster meaningful learning but also to improve the preparation of future chemistry teachers through the development of their assessment thinking. Talanquer has been honored with several awards, such as the Early-Career Teaching Award, the Five Star Teaching Award, Leicester and Kathryn Sherrill Creative Teaching Award, and the Henry and Phyllis Koffler Prize in Teaching. He has also been recognized with the James Flack Norris Award for the Outstanding Teaching of Chemistry and the Distinguished Achievement in Science Education Award. In 2015, Talanquer was recognized as the Arizona Professor of the Year. He received a B.S, an M.A., and a Ph.D. in chemistry, all from the Universidad Nacional Autónoma de México.

William F. Tate IV is the provost and executive vice president of academic affairs at the University of South Carolina (USC). He holds the USC Education Foundation distinguished professorship with appointments in sociology and family and preventive medicine (secondary appointment). Tate's research concentrates in four areas: (1) human capital development in STEM fields, (2) epidemiological models and geospatial applications with a focus on adolescent and child development and health outcomes, (3) social development of youth in the context of metropolitan communities, and

(4) stratification. Prior to joining the USC faculty, he served as dean and vice provost for graduate education at Washington University in St. Louis, where he held the Edward Mallinckrodt distinguished university professorship in arts and sciences. Before serving at Washington University in St. Louis, he held the William and Betty Adams chair at Texas Christian University and served on the faculty of the University of Wisconsin–Madison. He is a past president of the American Educational Research Association, where he was awarded fellow status. In addition, he was elected to the National Academy of Education. Tate earned his Ph.D. at the University of Maryland, College Park, where he was a Patricia Roberts Harris fellow.

Michael Torrence is a technology strategist. He has worked with higher education in many capacities and focused his expertise on research, adult education, student success, academic affairs, staff development, and distance learning. His other interests are Applied Learning within Open Education Resources, Virtual Reality, Augmented Reality, Mixed Reality, Automation, Robotics, Mechatronics, and Gamification as platforms for education, learning, and training business and industry to increase efficiency and scalability. Torrence is also an entrepreneurial business development professional with a Ph.D. in exceptional learning (literacy) from Tennessee Technological University.

Will Tyson is the associate professor of sociology at the University of South Florida. His research examines interpersonal and structural influences on STEM education and career pathways out of high schools, community colleges, and 4-year universities. Through this research, he examines how education facilitates life course transitions among students from various backgrounds. His current research focuses on school-to-work and work-to-school pathways of individuals enrolled in community college technician education programs in preparation for the 21st century high-technology workforce. He teaches courses in race and ethnicity, sport in society, and sociology of education. Tyson received his Ph.D. from Duke University.

Monique Umphrey is the president of Houston Community College Northeast. Prior to joining Houston Community College, she was the vice president of workforce innovation and the college-wide dean of information technology at the Center of Excellence, Cuyahoga Community College. In 2014, she immediately started implementing ways to improve the college's computer networking and programming educational tracks and planned for expansions into areas including cybersecurity, data analytics, cloud computing, and the Internet of Things. A new degree in cybersecurity as well as new certificates in data analytics were launched. Her goal was to unite and leverage the strengths of existing academic offerings and workforce development training to optimize career and education opportunities for Tri-C students. Umphrey was selected into the inaugural class of the Aspen Presidential Fellowship for Community College Excellence, a rigorous, 10-month executive leadership program for aspiring Community College presidents led by the Aspen Institute and the Stanford Educational Leadership Initiative. She has more than 20 years of information technology experience, with more than 8 years of leading large-scale projects at Fortune 500 companies. She also was an adjunct instructor in information systems management and is certified for both online and classroom teaching. Umphrey earned a B.A. in computer information systems and an M.S. from Middle Tennessee State University, and a doctorate of management from the University of Maryland.

Monica Van is a student at the University of California, San Diego (UCSD) obtaining her B.S. in cognitive sciences. As an active UCSD student, she is a research assistant in the Early Learning & Cognition Lab. She has helped organize the TEDxUCSD for 2 years, contributed to projects with Global TIES UCSD, and interned with the Qualcomm Institute-UCSD Division of Calit2. Van is one of the Idea Competition winners for the Symposium on Imagining the Future of Undergraduate STEM Education.

Suzanne L. Weekes is the incoming executive director of the Society for Industrial and Applied Mathematics and is currently the associate dean of undergraduate studies and professor of mathematical sciences at Worcester Polytechnic Institute (WPI). As dean, she is focused on the undergraduate research enterprise at the university to continue to advance WPI's mission to create, to discover, and to convey knowledge at the frontiers of academic inquiry for the betterment of society. Her mathematical interests are in numerical methods for differential equations including applications to spatio-temporal composites and cancer growth, and she is also involved in many initiatives connecting the academic mathematics community to mathematics and statistics work done in business, industry, and government. Weekes is co-founder and codirector of the national Preparation for Industrial Careers in Mathematical Sciences Program and the Mathematical Sciences Research Institute Undergraduate Program. She is the recipient of the 2019 Humphreys Award for Mentoring from the Association for Women in Mathematics and the 2020 Haimo Award for Distinguished College or University Teaching of Mathematics from the Mathematical Association of America. She serves on the Science Policy committees of both the American Mathematical Society and the Society for Industrial and Applied Mathematics. She is on the board of governors of the Transforming Postsecondary Education in Mathematics initiative. Weekes received a B.S. in mathematics from Indiana University, and a Ph.D. in mathematics and scientific computing from the University of Michigan, and did her post-doctoral work at Texas A&M University.

Robin Wright is the director of the Division for Undergraduate Education at the National Science Foundation (NSF). She is at NSF on a temporary assignment from the University of Minnesota's Department of Biology Teaching and Learning, for which she was the founding head. She previously served as associate dean for faculty and academic affairs in the College of Biological Sciences and as professor of genetics, cell biology, and development. At Minnesota, she helped to develop the Nature of Life Orientation Program and has been a leader in development of Foundations of Biology, an innovative, team-based introductory biology course for biological sciences majors. She served on the Education Committee of the American Society for Cell Biology and as chair of the Education Committee for the Genetics Society of America. She was a member of the Executive Committee for the Howard Hughes Medical Institute/National Academies of Science-sponsored Summer Institute on Biology Education and the National Academies' Scientific Teaching Alliance. During this work, she was named as a National Academies Biology Education Mentor for 14 consecutive years. She was elected as a fellow of the American Association for the Advancement of Science and received the Elizabeth Jones Award for Excellence in Undergraduate Education from the Genetics Society of America. Wright received a B.S. in biology from the University of Georgia and a Ph.D. in biological sciences from Carnegie-Mellon University.